Think Like a Publisher

TH!NK
LIKE A
PUBLISHER

RANDY DAVILA

Hierophant publishing

Cover design by Adrian Morgan
Cover art by Shutterstock
Text design by Steve Amarillo

Hierophant Publishing
8301 Broadway, Suite 219
San Antonio, TX 78209
888-800-4240
www.hierophantpublishing.com

If you are unable to order this book from your local
bookseller, you may order directly from the publisher.

Library of Congress Control Number: 2013945700

ISBN 978-1-938289-16-3

10 9 8 7 6 5 4 3 2 1

Printed on acid-free paper in the United States

*For my beautiful wife Rachel,
who always encourages me to pursue
my passions and to follow my heart.*

So the writer who breeds more words than he needs
is making a chore for the reader who reads.

—DR. SEUSS

Contents

Introduction

Writing a book will change you.

As a matter of personal accomplishment, it is unparalleled. My friend and fellow author Jacob Nordby says, "Holding up your completed book to the world is a watershed moment in your life." I couldn't agree more.

Creating a good book requires the intersection of four things: art, inspiration, craft, and marketing. Many of the writers I meet have a good start on the art and inspiration, but they need improvement in the departments of craft and marketing. If one of your goals is that your book reach as many people as possible, you will have to hone your talents on all four fronts. And if you want to make a living at publishing, you will really have to develop what I call the Author Business Model.

But before we delve into the nuts and bolts of the publishing world, I would like to thank you for picking up your pen, or more likely sitting behind your computer, and writing your book. You see, I have had the pleasure of working with authors from around the globe, both well-published and not-so-well-published, and the one thing they all have in common is that through this sacred craft of writing every one of them is attempting to make the world a better place (even if they may not realize it).

Whether you are writing a self-help book, a history book, a memoir, a novel, or a book in any other genre, the goal of a writer is to educate and entertain the reader, and in so doing contribute to the betterment of humanity. The world needs people like you, so I thank you for showing up.

Whether your book finds an audience here and abroad or you share it with just a few loyal readers, know that your writing will help at least one person—you. Writing is by definition a creative endeavor, one that energizes the mind and nourishes the soul. Although some authors don't realize this at first, writing is one of those conscious creation activities that makes us feel alive, and that's why we do it!

So by writing, whether you are conscious of it or not, you help others and yourself. This is why I often say that every book ever written, in some capacity and regardless of genre, is a self-help book.

A quick peek at history shows that what we are doing as authors does matter, that we are making the world a better place. We are privileged to live in the most literate time in the history of humanity, and literacy and education are inextricably linked. More people have the ability to read today than at any point in our past, and the collective education of this planet has never been higher. Undoubtedly we still have a long way to go, but much of our progress has been made through sharing ideas, and those ideas are recorded in books . . . books that would not exist without the authors who wrote them.

What a debt of gratitude we owe the authors who have come before us, who were brave enough to publish new ideas that expanded our thinking even when they were unpopular or posed a great risk to the writer's reputation. While there are countless examples of this type of heroism in authorship, one person who comes to mind is Dr. Brian L. Weiss, author of the international best-selling book on reincarnation titled *Many Lives, Many Masters: The True Story of a Prominent Psychiatrist, His Young Patient, and the Past-Life Therapy That Changed Both Their Lives.*

With degrees from Columbia University and Yale Medical School, Dr. Weiss was the head of the psychiatry department at the Mount Sinai Medical Center in Miami Beach when he wrote *Many Lives, Many Masters*. Dr. Weiss had much to lose when he began writing about the subject of past-life therapy in the mid-1980s. Well respected by his peers in traditional psychiatry, by his own admission Dr. Weiss had no use for "alternative" methods of treatment like past-life regression therapy. But then something happened to change all of that. While using hypnosis to help recall traumatic childhood memories, one particular patient went back "beyond" her childhood, remembering a total of eighty-six previous lives over the course of her months-long treatment. Although Dr. Weiss was very skeptical at first, the healing benefits this patient experienced as a result of excising past-life traumas, combined with the knowledge she received about Weiss's own life from "masters on the other side," convinced him that reincarnation was real and that past-life regression therapy could be a useful healing tool.

Despite the objection of many peers in the mainstream medical community, Dr. Weiss made the bold decision to risk his credibility and his career when he decided to publish his findings in a book. No one could have predicted, least of all Dr. Weiss, that the book would go on to sell millions of copies, bring reincarnation and past-life regression therapy into the spotlight, and change so many people's lives in the process.

In the genre of fiction, there are numerous examples of books that use storytelling to not only entertain readers but also challenge existing societal beliefs. Dan Brown's 2003 novel *The Da Vinci Code* not only captivated millions of readers with its suspenseful twists and turns but also reintroduced the idea of the divine feminine and its influence on mainstream Christianity. The firestorm that ensued after its publication was notable, to say the least.

These are but two examples, and there are numerous others as well, that we authors are a courageous folk. We put our hearts onto paper, risking the ridicule of critics and sometimes even our financial stability all in an effort to share our ideas with the world. Now comes the challenging part, and the likely reason you are reading this book: *What can you do as an author to help your book reach the widest possible audience and make the biggest impact on the world?*

Well, the good news is that there are many, many things you can do to help accomplish this goal. And that is the purpose of this book, to educate you, the author, about the essential steps necessary to reach as many readers as you can. As you will see in the following pages, there is so much more to being an author than just writing a book and either submitting it to a traditional publisher or self-publishing. At the conclusion of this book, my hope is that you will understand why I often say, "Being a good writer is one thing; being a well-published author is something else entirely."

What Is Success?

If you notice, I have not yet used the term "successful." I have not said, "Do this and make your book a success." Before I begin stating things such as "make your book successful," the first thing I want you to do is evaluate your definition of success.

Many first-time authors define a successful book as one that sells thousands if not millions of copies and earns the title "best seller." (We will discuss more about "best seller" claims and definitions in Tip #21.) And you can be sure that as a publisher my hope is that every book we produce will sell thousands if not millions of copies. But before we go any further, we must ask ourselves: Is the number of copies a book sells the only metric in determining if it is "successful"?

Not by my definition, and when you are done reading this, I hope not by yours either. I would like to offer you a different set of metrics for determining whether a book is successful or not. Defining success in terms other than number of copies sold means considering a few things. First, do you as the author feel good about the contents of your book? Will you be proud to see your name on the cover? I hope that is the case for you, and if it's not, I would strongly encourage you to get your manuscript into the best possible shape before it goes to print, because once your book is "out there" it will take on a life of its own, one that you want to be proud of forever.

Second, does your book help or educate people? Does it add value to the lives of its readers? When someone is finished reading your book, will the information you have shared or the story you have told enhance that reader's life in some way?

To me, these criteria are far more important when it comes to calling a book successful than the number of copies sold.

Now I will prove it to you.

Looking back over your life, there have undoubtedly been a handful of books that had a big impact on your worldview and your individual perspective. Dare I suggest that some of these books were even life-changing? On your list of favorite books I bet there is at least one, if not more than one, which you could hold up in the middle of a crowded shopping mall, scream out the title, and no one would have ever heard of it. In short, this book was important to you and your journey in life, but when compared to other books, it is relatively unknown.

At the same time, I am sure you can think of a time when you picked up a widely publicized best seller with great anticipation, only to find out that you couldn't get through the first chapter. Yet this book has sold millions of copies, and by that measurement, it is clearly a success.

In hindsight, which of these two books was more "successful" to *you*?

I hope this little exercise illustrates that success should not be measured simply by the numbers of copies sold. Furthermore, my experience with authors, including the widely published variety, is that if your only metric of success is the number of copies sold, then, ultimately, no number of copies will be enough. So please remember when I use the term "successful" throughout the rest of this book, I mean far more than just the number of copies sold.

How to Use This Book

In an effort to make the tips here easier to understand and implement, I am categorizing them under three topics: editorial, marketing, and business (dollars and cents). The information shared in these tips will overlap categories in many cases. Remember that ultimately the categories themselves merge into one final product: your completed book.

Some tips presented here are short, some tips are long; all are important. I strongly encourage you to read every tip and look for its application in your own development as an author, even if you feel you have "mastered" that particular tip or category. In my experience dealing with authors, it's often the areas they dismiss, saying, "This is not applicable to me," that end up being the ones they need the most help in. So if you find yourself skimming a section, try slowing down. Consider if there's a way this *might* apply to you.

This book is intended to help both nonfiction and fiction authors alike, as much of the information I am sharing applies to both genres. In many cases, I will make distinctions as to how this would apply for a fiction author versus a nonfiction author, but only when such a distinction is necessary. In making some of my points I have used real-life examples from my own publishing house, which specializes primarily in the self-help category. However you can be sure that the tips I present in this book can be applied to virtually all books, regardless of your particular genre or category.

While the publishing world can seem daunting at first, my hope is that by the time you reach the end of this book the "dawn will break and shine a light over the whole," providing you with a solid foundation for creating a book that you feel good about and that reaches the widest possible audience. In so doing, you will have created a successful book and made the transition from "writer" to "author."

Lastly, I want to make clear that the information presented here is important regardless of whether you intend to submit your manuscript to a traditional publisher or you self-publish. If you go with a traditional publisher, they will appreciate your overall understanding of the business. As a publisher, it's always easier for me to work with an author who understands why I do the things I do, and what I need from them to make a book successful. Should you go the self-publishing route, the knowledge here will be especially invaluable and can act as a guide for making your entry into the world of publishing a rewarding endeavor on both a personal and financial level.

In summary, one of the best things you can do for yourself as an author is to become educated about the publishing industry. You will want to know as much as you can about the publishing business from the perspective of writer, promoter, and salesperson for your book. Because as you will see in the following chapters, in today's publishing world, you need to be all three.

* * * * *

TIP

1

· · · · ·

Editorial, Marketing, and Business

A New Look
at an Old Business

The publishing world has changed, and the authors who are successful have changed with it. For you authors committed to getting a book deal from a traditional publisher, I have news for you: The days of just writing a manuscript, sending it to your publisher, and then going home to sit on your couch are long, long gone.

The same is true for authors who plan to self-publish. It surprises me how many authors who choose self-publishing think that all they have to do is get their book into print, list it on Amazon, and somehow it will magically "take off." It actually takes a whole lot more to make a book successful in today's publishing world. Why is this so? Lets take a look and find out.

Twenty years ago, if you wanted to buy a book, how did you do that? It was easy. You went into a bookstore, proceeded to the appropriate section, and chose a book from the limited number they had on their limited shelf space. This was effectively your only option!

In the publishing days of yesteryear, if you were one of the relatively small number of lucky authors to be published you were almost assured that your book would sell to some degree, as there were far fewer books being published. Limited shelf space meant that just the very act of getting your book into a bookstore almost assured you a certain number of sales!

In today's Information Age, the method by which readers find and buy books has changed in incredible ways. I am not just referring to *how* we buy books on Amazon. com, BN.com, or other e-tailers; *which* books we choose to buy has changed too.

Rather than going to a bookstore to pick from a limited number of titles on a particular subject, more and more readers use the Internet to research a topic and books before making a buying choice. Readers' choices are influenced by which books come up first in search results, reader reviews, and competitive pricing. Combine this with the fact that advancements in technology have made it easier and less costly for traditional publishers to bring more titles into print, and it's no wonder the number of books available today is in the millions. These same technological advancements have led to the creation of a new billion-dollar industry within the book business: self-publishing.

So compared to even just a few years ago, more books are coming to market than ever before, and the way in which readers select and purchase books has drastically changed, too. Overall, I think these are good changes for authors and readers. We have access to new voices that in years past would not have been heard, and readers have access to ideas they would otherwise never have been exposed to. But this also means that authors and publishers have to work harder than ever to create the best books possible, promote them effectively, and come up with unique ways to sell them!

• • • • •

Marketing

Author Platform: What It Is and Why You Need One

With more books being published than ever before, it takes a lot of marketing and promotion by the author and publisher to get readers to choose your book over all the others. So now, more than ever, an author's *platform* is vital to the sales success of the book.

· · · · ·

What is an author platform? This is one of the most commonly asked questions at my author workshops. An author's "platform" refers to the people who are already familiar with you and your ideas and will be willing and ready to purchase your book as soon as it is published. This is often referred to as your "tribe," or what I like to call your "home team."

Breaking this down even further, when I am considering publishing a manuscript and it comes time to evaluate an author's platform, I look at the *who* and the *how*. The "who" is the people who are already in your tribe and are familiar with you and your ideas because you are connecting with them on a regular basis. The "how" is how you are connecting with these people. Do you hold workshops and seminars? Do you have a strong Internet presence via your own website, blog, and/or social media websites? Do you have a large email list and do you regularly send out electronic newsletters or other communications? These are just a few examples of *how* an author can connect with those on his or her home team.

Sometimes your profession comes with a built-in platform. For instance, ministers, teachers, radio show hosts, or public figures are naturally communicating with an audience nearly every day. But for most authors that's just not the case.

In this book we'll cover many of the ways you can build your platform as an author, but first let's look at some real-life examples so you can see exactly what I mean by author platform and how it relates to selling your book.

On a grand scale, take a talk show host like Jon Stewart, host of *The Daily Show,* a political satire that airs on Comedy Central. His viewers are the "who," the people listening to him, and his show represents the "how," or how he connects with them. If Jon Stewart writes another book, the people who are most likely to buy it are his viewers. He can use his show to tell them about the book and ask them to buy it (and he surely will). Again, this is an extreme example, because you don't need to be a famous talk show host to have an effective platform.

Hierophant Publishing author Sunny Dawn Johnston, who penned *Invoking the Archangels: A Nine-Step Process to Heal Your Body, Mind, and Soul,* steadily and consistently built her platform over time by doing lectures, workshops, and teleclasses and creating an online social networking presence. (You can visit her at www.sunnydawnjohnston.com to see an example of a very effective author website.) She was also vigilant about doing radio interviews with any show she could, regardless of their media reach. She was careful to collect email addresses of those she spoke with about her ideas whenever possible. The result was that by the time her book came out she had built a nice platform, and her book has sold very well.

We will have lots of tips about creating and building your platform in the pages that follow, because that is an integral part of getting your book to as many people as possible. But before we leave this subject, one more note on platform building. To be effective, your book topic should match your platform following.

For instance, Jon Stewart has written comedic books on the history of American politics, which matches his platform perfectly. Sunny Dawn Johnston is a psychic medium and angel communicator, and her platform is built around this role. Her book is about angel communication, so this matches perfectly.

Occasionally I meet authors who have a decent platform but their book's topic does not correspond with the reason people are listening to them. For example, what if Jon Stewart had written an academic book on the origin of pedagogy? Or what if Sunny Dawn Johnston had written a book on auto mechanics? In both cases, their current platforms would have been of little help in the selling of their books.

When I discuss the importance of an author's platform at my workshops, invariably one attendee will bring up a now famous book or two that was written by an author who was completely unknown prior to the book's publication. While this can and does happen, it is by far the exception and not the rule. I want you to realize that for the vast majority of authors, a strong platform is a big part of creating a widely read book in the modern publishing world, and this is true of both fiction and nonfiction alike.

Platform can be so important that in some cases a publisher will actually reach out to someone with a good platform and ask them if they want to write a book, instead of the other way around! The truth be told, I have made those calls myself!

This is the power of platform. If you already have a large number of people listening to you and your ideas, that's wonderful news for your career as an author. If you don't yet have a strong platform, it's time to begin building one, and many tips in this book will show you how.

• • • • •

Editorial

Focus, Focus, Focus: Know the Purpose of Your Genre and Stick to It

On a macro level, there are only two types of books, fiction and nonfiction, with numerous categories underneath them (nonfiction: self-help, business, philosophy, etc.; fiction: young adult, romance, historical, etc.).

· · · · ·

The primary purpose of nonfiction is to educate or share information. The primary purpose of fiction is to entertain. Now, I realize that some of the best nonfiction books also entertain, and some of the best fiction books also educate, but these are secondary goals and should remain secondary in your mind as your write your manuscript.

You would be surprised at the number of submissions we receive each year that violate this basic rule.

For nonfiction authors, you must remember as you write that your future readers will be picking up your book to learn something. Consequently, including superfluous information, going off on tangents, and the like are not helpful to your reader and diminish the value of your book. This is especially true in today's publishing world where nonfiction books are very topic specific. As you write, be sure to ask yourself if what you are about to put on the page furthers your cause of educating the reader on your topic. If the answer is no, then you need to seriously question whether or not it should be in your book.

Unfortunately, this type of problem finds its way into books by traditional publishers. Let me share with you an example. A friend recently gave me his review on a book he read about the basics of Buddhism. He was unfamiliar with Buddhism and wanted to learn more, and the book's title and back cover text indicated that it would teach him about this Eastern religion's basic tenets. I had actually heard of this particular book myself but hadn't read it, so I was looking forward to hearing his take on it.

"It was just OK, an average read," he offered.

"How so?" I asked.

"Well, I did learn a few things about Buddhism, but I

had to wade through pages and pages of this guy's personal story to get to it," he replied.

Aha! And here we have a case in point for the need to remain focused. The author of this particular book had included a lot of his own personal journey, and because it was presented as a nonfiction informational book about the basics of Buddhism, my friend was disappointed. He picked up a nonfiction book about Buddhism to learn more about the topic of Buddhism (imagine that!), and what he got was a book that contained a good portion of memoir and not enough about the topic advertised. Perhaps you have had a similar experience of picking up a book that was advertised to be about one topic, only to find that the author spent a lot of time telling you about something else too, and that made the book less appealing.

This is a very common problem for first-time authors, especially in the self-help genre, because as you struggle with the craft of writing, it is easy to write about the one topic you know best: you! And while there is nothing inherently wrong with relying on your personal experience to support your ideas, in a nonfiction teaching book you want to be sure to write primarily about your ideas and use your story to support those ideas, instead of the other way around. You don't want to fall into the trap of writing about your own personal experience just because it is comfortable and easy for you to do.

If you are a nonfiction author, remember that the purpose of your book is to convey information and educate the reader. (That's why they picked up your book!) You consider yourself an expert on a particular topic, and now it's time to act like it. (Or perhaps I should say write like it!)

With fiction, a common problem I see is that the author has an agenda. They have ideas about the way the world is, or how they think it should be, or other information they wish to share, and they impose those ideas and information on the reader throughout the story. Remember that readers pick up fiction primarily to be entertained. For many, fiction offers an escape from everyday life, a chance to live in someone else's world for a few hours. Now, great fiction books educate their readers and have something to say about the world and the human condition; I am certainly not disputing that. However, you will notice that in great fiction, these ideas are always derived from the story and are deftly interwoven into the tale. As a fiction author once said, "Teaching in this way is akin to slipping a bonus gift into the reader's pocket during his or her journey through the book." Educating the reader is not intrusive on the story.

Fiction writer, before you pen your next sentence, ask yourself if what you are about to write moves your story along, or if you trying to "teach" the reader something. If it's the latter, remember that if you teach in an obvious way, your reader will probably not appreciate it. They may feel they are being lectured, or even deceived.

An excellent example of combining a compelling story with teaching is the Percy Jackson & the Olympians young adult adventure series by Rick Riordan. Maybe you're familiar with the first, and most popular, book in the series, *The Lightning Thief*. These novels follow the adventures of young Percy Jackson, a modern-day hero whose character is based on the Greek demigod Perseus, as he trots the globe battling the forces of evil. Readers have devoured these action-packed books since publication.

But Riordan, a former middle school teacher, does something extremely clever along the way. He uses the series to teach his readers all about Greek mythology in a way that is not boring or textbook-ish. This is because the story is dominant throughout the novel and the teachings are secondary. Nonfiction books about Greek mythology received a huge boost in sales after the release of the Percy Jackson series, and those lucky authors have Rick Riordan to thank for that.

So remember, a nonfiction book's primary purpose is to educate, and a fiction book's primary purpose is to entertain. These conventions should be respected by all authors, as readers have come to expect it and will be very unforgiving in their reviews of your book if you do not. The memoir is an exception to this rule. From a writing standpoint, the memoir is the bridge between fiction and nonfiction. Because while the information you are sharing is true (you, as the author, are stating, "these things happened to me!"), it is your story that you are telling for the reader, and they will only stay with you if your story is told in a compelling, intriguing manner and entertaining throughout. That's why the best memoirs are said to "read like a novel." In a memoir, you are taking the reader on a journey, and while you can certainly teach them something along the way, in the end, it's all about your story. An excellent example of this is Elizabeth Gilbert's best-selling book *Eat, Pray, Love.*

• • • • •

Marketing

What's in a Name? Only Everything

If your book is to reach a wide audience, it is nearly impossible to overestimate the importance of a good title. I have seen poorly written books sell pretty darn well simply because the title was so promising. And I have seen what I think are good books languishing on the shelves in part due to a poor title.

· · · · ·

When submitting your manuscript to a traditional publisher, a good title can help catch the attention of the editorial committee, signaling to them that you know what you're doing as an author. What are the critical elements of a good title? For nonfiction, it's simple: description. A good title for a nonfiction book should absolutely describe what the reader could expect to learn from the book as well as possible. If it is also catchy and engaging, that's a wonderful bonus. But never sacrifice description in order to be witty. This also applies to your subtitle, which should complement the main title in an effort to accurately describe the contents of your book.

For instance, if a potential reader has to read your book to understand or get the meaning of your title, *then you need a new one.* Chances are they won't ever get to discovering the meaning of your title because they won't be intrigued enough to read the book.

For some reason, probably because we are so close to it, authors are often the worst people to title their own work. (That goes for me as well, as I left the final decision on the title of this book to my staff.) If you go with a traditional publisher, they will make sure your book is well-titled. But as I said earlier, it helps to have the best title you can when sending in your submission. If you self-publish, coming up with a title is your responsibility.

As I'm writing this, there is a book on my desk called *Pearls of Wisdom: 30 Inspirational Ideas to Live Your Best Life Now* by Jack Canfield, et al. (Hierophant Publishing 2012). Based on the descriptive nature of this title, you should have a darn good idea what to expect from the book.

Let me share with you an example of how a title can

change everything about a book. A few years ago, I decided to publish a book that had previously been self-published. The book was well-written and contained some very interesting information, but I didn't care for the title—*The New Bridge*. Take a moment to think about all the possible topics a book called *The New Bridge* could be about. Is this a book on architecture? Relationships? Politics? You will be interested to know that I published the book under the title *The Extraterrestrial Answer Book: UFOs, Alien Abductions, and the Coming ET Presence* (Hampton Roads 2009).

Can you see now how the title makes all the difference? Now, in fairness to the author, the self-published version of the book had the subtitle *Planning for the Extraterrestrial Presence;* but this does not make up for a title that leaves the reader guessing as to the contents of the book.

For fiction, a good title is equally important, but the rules are a little different. Fiction authors have some room for creativity in a title that nonfiction authors don't have. While you want to be suggestive of the contents of the book, I think the more important goal of a good fiction title is to intrigue the potential reader, capture their imagination, and invite them to take the journey by reading your book.

A close friend of mine mentioned in the introduction, Jacob Nordby, accomplished this quite well. He self-published his novel *The Divine Arsonist: A Tale of Awakening*. Another example of a best-selling novel with a great title is *The Da Vinci Code* by Dan Brown.

Since memoir is a sort of bridge between fiction and nonfiction, I also suggest creating a title that is more intriguing, mimicking the fiction authors. Elizabeth Gilbert's *Eat, Pray, Love,* mentioned in a previous tip, accomplishes this goal quite well.

In summary, don't underestimate the importance of an effective title. Without it, an editor or potential reader is far less likely to be excited by, or even pick up, your book.

EXERCISE

Gather a group of friends who are familiar with your manuscript and your ideas, and have a brainstorming session on possible titles. Make sure you preface the exercise with this qualification: For nonfiction, the title needs to describe the contents of the book as accurately and completely as possible. For fiction, the title should be intriguing as well as suggestive of the contents of the book.

Many times a good title is the result of mixing and matching ideas from a variety of people in a brainstorming session like this, and this is true at traditional publishing houses, too.

• • • • •

Editorial and Marketing

Did I Mention the Importance of Focus?

Now it's time for part two on focus, because if your book lacks it, then there is very little chance, if any, that it will reach a wide audience.

O ne of the most common mistakes inexperienced authors make is trying to do too much in one book. This is especially true of first-time nonfiction authors, who often think they need to put *everything* they know into their first book. Not only does this dilute the focus of your current book, but it also leaves you little else to write about in the future!

In a later tip on what I call the Author Business Model, I will explain why you want to think about your career in publishing as one that encompasses more than one book. But for now, it's sufficient to say that in the modern publishing world where more books are coming to market than ever before and competition for readers has never been greater, it is vitally important that you write a very focused book.

For nonfiction, ask yourself, What is the one main idea you want readers to take away from your book? Be clear on what this is, and everything you write about in one way or another should relate back to that main idea. Of course, you will have many supporting ideas you will share, but it should all fall under the umbrella of your one big idea.

For fiction and memoir authors, ask yourself, What is the overarching story line that moves my book along? This story is the yarn with which you thread the needle, and it sews up all the subplots throughout your book.

Sometimes an inexperienced author will write a book that spans two categories. This creates confusion not only in the mind of the reader but also the booksellers and media outlets that will cover you and your book. First, readers of nonfiction search for a book in one particular category; it is rare that you will find a reader who wants to learn about *this topic* and *that topic* in the same book. And second, bookstores will only put a book in one place. No publisher that I know of would present them a book and suggest they put it in two different categories in the same store. In addition, the world of media as a whole has become very niche. When you or your publisher approach magazines, newspapers, blogs, TV, or radio outlets for author interviews and book reviews, it needs to be very clear who the book's target market is. This will increase the chances of getting the book coverage.

Now let's look at how this applies in the world of fiction. Say an author is writing a novel that could go in romance *and* mystery. This is not a strong position to take. While a romance could be an element of any good mystery novel, and mystery is certainly implied in most romances, it should be clear which story line is dominant—romance, or mystery? That will determine the book's category. Readers know that romance novels have a certain "feel" to them, as do mystery books, and a new author will do well to give the reader what they want.

Here is a real-life example of what I mean. In one of my author workshops, I was presented a book idea by an author who felt that her book should be placed in two different categories. She had written a self-help book about how to recover from the death of a loved one *and* the importance of eating organic food. Most of the other students quickly realized the perils of tying these two subjects together in one book, as the only common denominator in each subject appeared to be the author's interest and stated expertise in both.

Now, including both experiences may have been fine if she were writing her memoir, but this author was insistent that she were writing a nonfiction informational book on how to move through the grief of a departed loved one and the benefits of going all organic. And while the perils of combining these two subjects into one book was obvious to almost everyone else in the class, it absolutely was not clear to this author. And herein lies another problem: When it comes to staying focused in your writing, many authors can see the flaws in other people's work, but they find it very difficult to see the flaws in their own.

This is an exaggerated example, but in some cases the split may not be so apparent. Let's say, for instance, you have written a book to help people navigate through the problems that occur at the intersection of relationships and money. For a book like this, the first question would be: Does it belong in the self-help/relationships category, or does it belong in personal finance? The answer depends largely on how the book is written.

You could write a book on personal finance that cites relationships as a continual source of financial trouble, or you could write a book on relationships that shows how the stress of money is one of the top reasons they fall apart. The former book would be categorized in personal finance, and the latter would go in self-help.

The point I want to make here is that in the rare event that a book could have two intersecting subject matters, one topic should clearly be the primary focus, and the other should be clearly secondary. Once you make that choice, stick to it throughout your manuscript.

I can tell you with a fair amount of certainty that if you submit a book proposal to a traditional publishing house and claim that your book could or should be in two or more categories, the chances of it getting accepted will fall dramatically.

As I said in the introduction, writing is art and inspiration; but to create a successful book you will also need craft and marketing. Focus is a big part of the craft, and the foundation of any good book, so make sure yours has it.

EXERCISE

Go to a local bookstore (the bigger the better) and see how it categorizes books on the shelves. Then decide where your book would go in that particular store. For some of you, this will be an easy exercise, and that's great. For others, you might hear yourself saying, my book could go here *or* there. That makes me very nervous, as it may be a sign that you are trying to do too much in one book.

· · · · ·

TIP

6

· · · · ·

Marketing

The Time to Start Building Your Platform Is *Now*

Remember, your author platform refers to those people who are already familiar with you and your ideas and are ready to buy your book when it's published.

· · · · ·

One of the biggest misconceptions new authors have in this department sounds something like this: "Sure, Randy, I understand the importance of a good platform. I'll start building mine as soon as the book comes out."

Wrong! The last thing you want to do is wait for your book to come out before you get started on this vital component of publishing success. You want to begin building your platform as soon as possible, preferably well before your book comes out!

There are two primary reasons for this. First, the people on your home team are the ones who are familiar with you and your ideas, and as a result, they should be primed and ready to buy your book when it comes out. In many cases, these are the only people who are willing and ready to buy your book on its publication date if you are a first-time author, so they are critical to a successful book launch.

Publishers and authors both benefit from a fast start to a book. When a book takes off early, not only does it provide you and the publisher with a sense of accomplishment, but it can also make it easier to get publicity. An early success can raise the book's profile in the minds of the bookstore buyers (a buyer is responsible for choosing the books and the quantities that end up on the bookstore shelves). Another obvious benefit to a fast start is that both you and the publisher will realize a quicker financial return on your investment, and a fast start is almost impossible without a strong author platform.

Second, not only will your home team buy your book on its publication date, but if they like it, they will refer your book to others. This referral process is vital, because even in this high-tech world of information on demand the number one way a book sells is still by word of mouth.

These word-of-mouth referrals are what I call second generation sales. First generation sales are when someone buys your book because they had direct contact with you. Second generation sales are when that person tells their friends and family and acquaintances about your book and someone in that circle buys it. In an ideal scenario, first generation sales will lead to second generation sales. It will take both for your book to reach a wide audience.

The goal of publishing any book is to get it into as many hands as possible, which at first are the hands of those on the home team. Because if they read it, like it, and refer it to enough people, then the book will reach a tipping point where it begins to sell more and more copies by means of second generation sales than first generation sales. And now you are well on your way to success.

Future tips will be devoted exclusively to platform building with specific instructions on how to do just this, but the main takeaway from this tip is: *Don't wait to start building your author platform!*

HOMEWORK

Platform building takes time, and I suggest that—starting today—you commit to spending a certain number of hours each week just on building your platform. Doing so is a very practical application of this step, one that will pay dividends over the long haul. The more hours per week you can spend on platform building the better, but even if that is only one or two, the benefits of such consistent and regular work will be apparent once your book is published, and this is true whether you go with a traditional publisher or self-publish.

· · · · ·

Editorial and Marketing

Target Your Market

In my author workshops, I often ask participants, "Who is your book for?"

Unfortunately, one of the most common answers I get is, "Everyone!"

● ● ● ● ●

While I understand and appreciate the spirit of that answer, let me be clear that *no book* is for "everyone." There has never been a book in the history of the world that satisfies this audacious claim. Please make sure that as you are building your platform and writing your book you stay focused on the realistic group of people who may ultimately buy and read it. The key word here is *realistic*.

For example, I was once coaching an author who had a very strong platform as a psychic animal communicator. Her book promised readers a step-by-step guide on how they could develop their own psychic skills to communicate with their pets. In her proposal, she indicated that her book was for *all* pet owners and cited the number of pet owners in the United States, how much they spent on their furry friends each year, and anticipated high sales as well as a high marketing budget for the book based on the multibillion dollar pet industry.

Now what was immediately clear to me, and I hope to you too, was that this book was *not* meant for all pet owners. It was a book for pet owners who are also interested in communicating psychically with their pets. That eliminates a lot of the pet owners!

Let's stay with this example for a moment longer. By better understanding who her readers are, this author can focus her writing and her platform building to this targeted group. From the editorial side, she can stay focused on writing a book for people who are already open and interested in psychic communication, and who have pets. In so doing, she won't waste time and slow down the book by including chapters or sections that argue for the validity of psychic communication. (This would only be necessary if her book were for *all* pet owners, many of whom would need convincing.) Instead, only those readers who already believe that one can and should psychically communicate with a pet will be inclined to pick up this book for the steps on how to do so. So in this case, targeting your readers accurately helps you to write a very focused book.

From the marketing side, spending promotional time and money to reach "all" pet owners would be a colossal waste of resources. The media world is very niche, and it is unlikely that a mainstream TV series, radio show, or publication for pet owners would pay any attention to a book like this. Yet, there are many media outlets that cover psychic phenomena that probably would be interested in this book.

Keeping your target readership group in mind is essential. This is true for nonfiction and fiction authors alike. Doing so allows you to focus your writing, platform building, and book marketing to the group most likely to receive it positively.

* * * * *

Editorial and Marketing

Know Your Hook

Take a moment to think about these questions:

What is your book about?

Why are you qualified to write your book?

What will someone gain, or how will they benefit from reading your book? (This is your hook.)

.....

These are the most important questions your potential readers will probably never ask. They are also some of the key items a potential publisher will be using to evaluate your manuscript and proposal, so as you talk about and otherwise promote yourself and your book, you had better include the answers to all three.

What Is Your Book About?

The first question may appear easy, but looks can be deceiving. Remember, the goal here is to tell readers *in as few words as possible* what they can expect to get out of your book. Take a moment to do this now.

EXERCISE

Complete the following statement in no more than two sentences:

My book is about _____

_____

_____

_____.

This is excellent practice not only for your real-life marketing efforts, but also for what is to come next in this book (hint!).

For example, we recently published Thérèse Amrhein Tappouni's book *The Gifts of Grief: Finding Light in the*

Darkness of Loss. If I were to answer the first question as the author of that book, I would say:

> My book is about recovering from a devastating loss, such as the death of a loved one, a financial catastrophe, or debilitating illness. It's a how-to guide for not only overcoming the intense pain that accompanies these tragedies but also finding the benefits, or "gifts," in them too.

For a fiction example, I will use my own novel, *The Gnostic Mystery.*

> My book is about a wealthy American man who is having a midlife spiritual crisis. He undertakes a pilgrimage to war-torn Jerusalem to reconnect with the faith of his childhood, but instead encounters the teachings of an ancient Christian sect called the Gnostics. The result of this encounter will shake the very foundation of his Christian faith.

Why Are You Qualified to Write Your Book?

Next let's discuss the importance of crafting your author biography. This is frequently overlooked by authors, but it is also of vital importance. Here is your opportunity to qualify yourself to potential readers, to cast yourself as an expert in a particular subject or a master storyteller.

When crafting your author bio, you only want to use things that will be helpful to the reader as it pertains to your book. For instance, if you are writing a self-help book about drug addiction and recovery, keep your focus on credentials and relevant experience. The fact that you hold the state record for the largest bass ever caught is impressive, but it does not belong in your author bio.

Using the same books as above, here are two examples of author bios.

The Gifts of Grief

Author Therèse Amrhein Tappouni knows the journey all too well. Having survived the tragic death of her eleven-year-old son, the loss of a thirty-six-year marriage, debilitating health issues, and, finally, bankruptcy, she found a way through grief that would add to her life rather than add to her sorrow. As a grief counselor and certified medical and clinical hypnotherapist, she brings both personal experience and professional training to bear as she leads readers through the darkest hours of their lives.

The Gnostic Mystery

Randy Davila has been a student of esoteric Christianity for many years. He graduated with distinction from the Classics, Philosophy, and Religion department at the University of Mary Washington in Virginia, where he cofounded and wrote for the award-winning publication *The Free Press*. His spiritual short stories have received the Place of Peace Award. This is his first novel.

How Does Your Book Benefit the Reader? (Your Hook)

Now for your "hook." Quickly defined, your hook is your unique angle; it's the payoff the reader receives for engaging your book, and it's what makes your book different from all the other books out there. The idea, as the moniker implies, is that your book's unique angle will hook potential readers or publishers, and prompt them to either buy or publish your book.

Your hook may include much of the same language as the previous two questions. Once you have answered those questions succinctly, your hook is usually much easier to articulate.

When thinking about your hook, imagine that you only have thirty seconds to tell a potential reader or publisher what makes your book unique and how they will benefit by reading it. Given the short time constraint, what exactly would you say? It's important to remember that your hook is intended for those in your target audience, not just any man or woman walking down the street. Those in your target audience should have some familiarity with your subject matter already.

Let's look at a couple examples.

The Gifts of Grief

My book is different from other grief books because despite the devastating loss of my eleven-year-old son, I found a way to transform my pain and suffering into gratitude and blessings. In this book, I offer a road map for others to do the same.

As you can see, your hook can include your qualifications as an author—and it should when that is helpful to your case.

Here's another example: In the introduction I mentioned Dr. Brian Weiss's book, *Many Lives, Many Masters*. The hook there is something like "a skeptical Ivy League doctor becomes a believer in past-life regression therapy when one of his patients remembers many previous lives while under hypnosis, right before his very eyes."

For fiction authors, remember that the hook is all about the story, and what it offers to readers who go on the journey. Consequently, your author bio may not be as important. Let's take a look at a hook for a novel.

The Gnostic Mystery

> Set in Jerusalem amidst the backdrop of the Palestinian-Israeli conflict, readers travel along with the protagonist through his own crisis of faith, and in the process they will be forced to question their own ideas about the origins of Christianity and the power of belief.

By working with these three questions, you can make the most compelling presentation to readers and publishers on what they can expect from you and your book, and why they should buy or publish it.

• • • • •

Editorial and Marketing

Pitch Your Book

Now it's time for a self-test.

• • • • •

The following exercise will help you make sure your book is focused, as well as provide a good outline to follow when talking about your book to a potential publisher or reader. I strongly suggest taking the time to write out your answers in the exercise below in as few words as possible.

EXERCISE[1]

1. The title of my book is _____.

2. This is a book about _____ (your specific topic).

3. It's for _____ (your target audience).

4. My book's hook is: _____. (What will readers take away from your book? How will they benefit? What makes your book unique?)

5. I am qualified to write this book because _____.

Now show your answers to four or five people and get their reactions. Remember, your main goal here is to accurately communicate the contents of your book in the shortest amount of time.

Why do I keep insisting on staying within the shortest amount of time? Because in many cases, that is all the time you have when it comes to talking about your book.

---

[1] This exercise is a modified version of one created by my friends at Red Wheel/ Weiser, LLC, and used here with permission.

Marketing

Most People Judge a Book by Its Cover

Like it or not, corporate bookstore buyers as well as readers almost always judge a book by its cover, so yours had better be good! If it's not, the chances of your book reaching a wide audience begin to fall dramatically.

• • • • •

By definition a cover is a work of art, so explaining what makes a good cover is more difficult than other tips in this book, but here goes: The cover of your book should match the spirit/tone of the contents as well as possible. The cover is also an opportunity to convey via images and colors that which you cannot or chose not to say directly in your title (sometimes for the sake of brevity).

For example, a little while back Hampton Roads published Linda Martella Whitsett's book, *How to Pray without Talking to God*. The cover designer apparently missed the initial memo describing the contents, tone, and style of the book, because when the first cover came back for approval, it arrived in very dark colors with big, bold, loud text which seemed to scream HOW TO PRAY WITHOUT TALKING TO GOD!

This would have been the perfect cover if Linda had written an in-your-face book that barked marching orders. But she is a Unity church minister who wrote a very gentle, comforting, and soul-nourishing book. Had we gone ahead with the first cover, we would have mislead the reader by indicating one thing graphically and delivering something entirely different in the pages inside. The final cover we went with has soft colors and a hummingbird on the front, which far more accurately matches the spirit of the book.

Another effective cover is Jack Canfield's *Pearls of Wisdom: 30 Inspirational Ideas to Live Your Best Life Now*. You'll see bright, uplifting colors and a big luminescent pearl. It completely matches the spirit of the text inside.

Also check out Sunny Dawn Johnston's *Invoking the Archangels*. For this cover, we put Sunny on the front, realizing that many people would buy her book as a result of seeing her in person, as she speaks to groups around the country on a regular basis. In addition, the teachings in the book are heavily supported by her personal experience, another reason to put her image on the cover.

On a side note about covers, Sunny had originally wanted the cover to have a graphic with angels so that it would appeal strongly to those in her niche. While that can be a good idea in many cases, I disagreed in this one. You see, Sunny's platform and following in the angel niche is so strong that people on the "home team" would buy her book even if it had a blank cover! That's how strongly they feel about Sunny and her message. But I wanted to give this book a chance to do more. The resulting cover is something that is very mainstream friendly and approachable to those who are just considering the idea that they could learn how to invoke archangels. In this case, a more general cover could do more to help sell the book to a mainstream audience.

Now let's look at how an effective cover can convey an idea or message to the reader that was not included in the title of the book. I was once coaching an author who was planning to self-publish her book that promised readers a step-by-step guide on surviving a hostile divorce. The book was very well written, and I particularly liked the title, with one exception.

It was clear to me that the book was written exclusively for women, but that wasn't indicated in the title. As a result, any man who bought the book to learn how to navigate a hostile divorce would feel cheated (no pun intended!). But her title was so good we feared that to try and add that this book was for women only in the text of the title would have taken away from its effectiveness. The solution became clear: the cover designer needed to make sure the art and color scheme conveyed to the reader that this was a book written for women only. This could be accomplished by making the primary color on the cover pink, or by including traditionally feminine graphics. This is an example of how a cover can be used to say what you couldn't (or didn't) say in the title.

If a traditional publisher publishes your book, they will handle the cover design. You as an author should be consulted, but the publisher will have the final say as a matter of contract in almost all cases. If for some reason the cover they provide fails the criteria I have set out in this chapter, point that out to them!

For those of you who choose to self-publish, you will have the final say in the selection of your cover, so it's vitally important for you to remember that a good cover conveys graphically to the reader what to expect from your book!

Lastly, I want to be clear that cover design is not an exact science. Take heart in knowing that experienced book publishing professionals often disagree strongly on cover concepts. Some of the most animated arguments I have seen at the office are over which should be the final cover of a book.

EXERCISE

Review the covers of books you have read that are published by traditional publishing houses. Keeping in mind what I have just told you about the cover needing to match the contents of the book, can you see where this is almost always the case with professionally published books?

• • • • •

TIP

11

Marketing

Using Social Media to Build Your Platform

I explained earlier that the publishing world has changed, in large part due to new technology. One of the benefits of this technology as it pertains to platform building is the proliferation of social media. For the first time in history, all authors, regardless of how famous or well published they are, can now communicate directly with their readership base through social media websites, as well as use these sites to create interest in their books and ideas.

•••••

As a new author, I consider social media an absolute must. Websites like Facebook, Twitter, LinkedIn, Pinterest, YouTube, and the like are fantastic vehicles to help build your platform and create interest in you and your book.

Why am I so insistent on this? Well, in addition to the points I have already raised, social media sites are either inexpensive or free. Next, there are literally over a billion people engaging regularly on these social network sites. The combination of these two factors means the investment you will make in social media is one of time, and if done properly, it can be time very well spent.

How you use social networking will be slightly different depending on whether you are writing fiction or nonfiction.

Social Media and Nonfiction Authors

For my nonfiction authors, you want to see Facebook and other social networking sites as a way of sharing your ideas with an open hand, presenting yourself as an expert on the topic, and building a community of followers that you can engage with about your ideas. This is the place to let your passion for your subject matter shine through.

Please note that I did *not* say: "Use social media websites as a way to sell your book." This is because few people will want to follow a page that is little more than a commercial or brochure for an author's book—especially an unknown author. People go to social media pages of authors for the same reason they pick up books: to learn something or to be entertained.

Consequently, you should be generous with your ideas and messages on these social networking sites. If you do this effectively, you will move people and they will want to learn more by buying and reading your book. You don't need to take my word for it, just look at the official Facebook page of almost any major nonfiction author and you'll see this is exactly what they do! They focus on sharing information, not selling books!

This is not to say that you can't make occasional posts encouraging people to purchase and read your book—you can and should do that, too—but the key word here is *occasional*, as the focus of your activities should be sharing information. In the world of social media, direct selling should be secondary to your sharing of information with an open hand, asking nothing for it in return.

Social Media and Fiction Authors

For fiction authors, the same rules of generosity apply, but the focus shifts from sharing information to providing enticing details about the plot, characters, and overall story of your book. I recommend sharing engaging quotes and excerpts, and you might also consider making the first chapter available for free online. Your goal is that readers will be intrigued enough by the tidbits and beginning of your story to be compelled to take the journey with you.

＊＊＊＊＊

Remember Tip #3, about being true to the focus of your genre? The primary purpose of nonfiction is to teach or share information, and the primary purpose of fiction is to entertain through an engaging story. This is true when you write your book, and it is also true as you build your platform via social media.

In summary, social networking sites can be very helpful as you spread awareness of your ideas or your story, and the long-term goal is to pique readers' interest enough to buy and read your book. But I repeat, *do not* just post something on these websites to the effect of "Buy my book!" as this approach rarely, if ever, is effective.

• • • • •

Business and Marketing

The Importance of E-books

E-books have gotten a lot of attention in the last few years. In this tip we will take a look at what all the hoopla is about, and the ways in which e-books can benefit you as an author.

In the publishing world, the term e-book refers to any book that comes in a digital format, whether that be on Amazon's Kindle, Barnes & Noble's Nook, the Sony Reader, Apple's iPad, or any other digital format.

As of this writing, nearly a quarter of book sales come from e-books, so you will want to be sure an electronic edition of your book is available on all the major platforms. If you go with a traditional publisher, they will take care of this for you automatically. If you self-publish, the vast majority of companies that provide self-publishing services also include creating an e-edition at no additional charge (be sure to confirm this with the company you choose, should you go this route).

Both the publisher and you as the author will receive revenue on every e-book sold. From a return on investment standpoint, I actually prefer e-books over printed books for a variety of reasons. First, an e-book will never be out of stock. Second, they are very inexpensive to create. I don't have to print and ship an e-book from a warehouse in Virginia all the way to a retail store in California so someone can buy it. And third, there are no returns with e-books; when it sells, it sells!

Occasionally, someone in one of my author workshops will confuse my role as a book publisher with that of a book printer, which I am not. In fact, no traditional publisher I know of also owns a printing press. As you can imagine, printers are not very enthusiastic about the growth of e-books.

One question I am often asked is, "Should I put out my book as an e-book only?" To me, if you are serious about your career as an author, the answer is almost always no. While currently almost 25 percent of books sold are e-books, and this number is growing, if you just publish your book in an electronic format you would be leaving about 75 percent of your potential readers in the dark. In addition, there is a notion in the minds of many readers that if your book is an e-book only, you are somewhat of a second-rate author, that perhaps your book "isn't worthy enough" to be printed. This is not true, but unfortunately some potential readers perceive e-books as being lesser than. If self-publishing an e-book is all you can afford, by all means do it. But if you want your book to reach as wide an audience as possible, an e-book alone is rarely a way to long-term success as an author.

Why Books Won't Go the Way of the CD or the DVD

While e-books will certainly continue to increase their market share as compared to printed books, I don't expect e-books will ever completely replace printed books the way downloading music and streaming movies have effectively replaced the CD and DVD.

The reason for the demise of the CD and DVD is that they were just a medium of information; they had no physical value in and of themselves. You listen to the songs and watch the TV screen in the same way, regardless of how the information arrives to your ears and eyes, whether it is by download or vinyl disk.

Not so for books. Many people prefer a physical book to an e-reader for a variety of reasons: they say it is easier on the eyes, they can scribble notes in the margins (although the functionality and readability of e-readers will continue to improve), and they have an attachment to the book as an object. Books are accessories in our homes, they can be beautiful, and culturally we have a longstanding romance with them.

Editorial and Marketing

Start Your Book with a Bang

We live in an age where consumers are accustomed to receiving information in record time and on demand. We see this reflected in the features from Amazon and other e-tailers that allow readers to "search inside this book" and read the first few pages. Or imagine you're browsing the books in a brick-and-mortar store. Do you ever flip open to the first paragraph and decide whether you want to buy the book based solely on that? Also, remember that more books are coming to market than at any time in history, giving readers more and more options. Given these conditions, starting your book with a bang is more important now than ever before.

This will mean different things to different authors, depending on whether you are writing fiction or nonfiction.

Starting Your Book with a Bang: Nonfiction

For nonfiction, a true master of the art of starting a book with a bang is Hampton Roads Publishing author Neale Donald Walsch. Neale wrote the Conversations with God series and numerous other books, several of which have made the *New York Times* Best Seller list.

If you don't have any of Neale's books, I suggest picking up some if for no other reason than to study how he begins them. Neale has a very strong writing voice that engages his readers from the opening paragraph. In addition, his books are all titled extremely well, and the first paragraph follows very logically from the title. Neale connects with the reader right away by acknowledging why they have picked up the book and offers a compelling roadmap of where the book is going and what the payoff is for the reader if they choose to take the journey with him. So far, several million readers have done so.

Starting Your Book with a Bang: Fiction

For fiction, begin your book whenever possible with action, or with your main character facing an intense moment or decision. This can draw your reader in and get them engaged in your story from the beginning. Look at modern-day authors like Dan Brown and Stephenie Meyer, who are experts at doing just this. There is no wait time with these authors—you are hooked from the beginning.

Many authors, especially first-time authors, have a tendency to ease into their thesis or story, and consequently they don't get to the point quickly enough. With first-time authors, sometimes the true beginning of their book starts five, ten, or even twenty pages into the manuscript. That's because it can take that long for new authors to find their voice and get into a groove. This is where a good editor will come in handy (discussed in a later tip), as he can help you see that the first few pages of your manuscript were for you only, and that your book actually starts somewhere after that.

In summary, it's hard to imagine a book that can't be made better by getting off to a fast start. In today's publishing world you often have just a few paragraphs to grab and keep your reader's attention. Despite this, so many authors don't do it. Make sure you are not one of them.

● ● ● ● ●

Editorial

Clarity Is Key, Except When It Isn't

One of your top jobs as an author is to be crystal clear for the reader. For nonfiction, this means not making the reader guess what your main points or arguments are. For fiction, this means helping the reader follow your story with ease.

Virtually every one of us has had the experience of reading a page in a book, getting to the bottom, and saying to ourselves, what in the heck is this author talking about? That is *not* the reaction you want for your book, especially in the modern publishing world.

Whether you are writing fiction or nonfiction, if a reader picks up your book and your story or teachings are hard to follow, it is very unlikely that they will continue reading it, as there are so many other books to choose from.

To me, the worst possible review of a book is when a reader says, "I couldn't get into it" or "I just couldn't finish it." I would rather the books I publish receive a scathing, horrible critique, where the reviewer vehemently disagrees with the ideas presented, because in that case one thing is clear: the reviewer finished it!

With more books coming to market than ever before, giving readers virtually unlimited choices, it is vital that you be able to articulate your ideas very clearly and succinctly.

There is only one exception to this rule. While your writing still needs to be very clear in fiction, some things should be left to the reader's interpretation. As the great Stephen King says, "Description begins in the writer's imagination, but should finish in the reader's." So in this sense, clarity is not key; but this should not be confused with writing unclear prose, which should never happen.

BONUS TIP

· · · · ·

Readers Love Anecdotes and Short Stories!

A story can be a very powerful teaching tool. Many best-selling authors use the device regularly, but aspiring authors would do well to take note of this technique, too. In fact, there was a "self-help teacher" who shared his message 2,000 years ago almost exclusively through the vehicle of story, also known as a parable. Later those parables were collected into a book that has since sold more copies than any other book in the history of mankind.

Readers love a simple story, and there is a tried-and-true format for a nonfiction chapter that goes like this:

1. Begin with a short story or anecdote that exemplifies the main idea of that chapter.

2. Explain your main idea in the middle section.

3. Conclude your chapter by referencing the story you cited initially as the proof of your main idea.

For my fiction authors, obviously the story is your main device. Occasionally a fiction author will use a short story or parable to make a point as well. For an excellent example of this, look no further than Paulo Coelho's *The Alchemist,* one of the best-selling novels of the last twenty years. In the opening pages, one of the main characters reads the parable of Narcissi, but changes the ending. The new version of this ancient story serves as a metaphor for one of the main ideas in the novel.

In short (pun intended!), don't overlook the value of a simple story or anecdote when making your point. Readers love them, and their effectiveness is well documented.

· · · · ·

Editorial

The Benefits of an Early Readers Group

Virtually every first-time writer who presents their book idea to me in my role as publisher says, "Those who have read my manuscript love it." And so I ask, "Who are those people?" The answer almost always begins with a spouse or significant other, parent, close friend, or even the author's children. While I am sure they do sincerely love your manuscript, I am willing to bet they also love you! Because of this, it's difficult, if not impossible, for most of them to remain objective when it comes to helping you with your writing.

•••••

While various authors and editors have different ideas on this subject, I am a big believer in having a group of "early readers" for your manuscript. This group of friends and family provides an invaluable service to you as an author: encouragement. That is something every writer needs, so be grateful that you have them in your corner to push you along the road of writing a book, especially on those days when you are having trouble finding the art and inspiration to continue.

That being said, your close friends and family shouldn't be the *only* people in your early readers group. If they are, you could be doing yourself and your manuscript a great disservice. Please allow me to explain.

I recommend having two other figures serving in your early readers group. First, find someone who will tell you what they think about your writing without any inhibitions. This person can tell you what parts of your manuscript need improvement, where you go off on tangents, where they feel you lack focus, what they like and dislike, etc. They are not in love with you, and they are not concerned about stroking your ego; they are only interested in helping you get better as a writer. By definition, this really can't be the person you go to sleep next to every night. This person could be a friend, coworker, or in some cases even a family member, but the main requirement for this reader is that you respect and value their opinion, and you know they will be uninhibited in their comments and criticism of your work.

This next person I suggest adding may be harder to find, but they are the most important person in your early readers group. This is the person who knows very little, if anything, about your ideas (if nonfiction) or story line/plot (if fiction/memoir) prior to reading your manuscript. This also means that you haven't spoken to them about the contents of your book. In many cases, your closest friends and family have already heard about your ideas or story line because you have explained it verbally. Consequently, if your writing is unclear, they may be able to subconsciously "fill in the blanks" on the parts that would otherwise be confusing. Someone who has no experience with your writing or book's content can tell you right away where they get lost or what portions of your writing need clarification, and that feedback is *invaluable*.

When I was writing my novel, the person I chose for this role was a distant cousin (she actually filled both of the above roles for me). I knew she loved to read, and I respected her opinion, but since we didn't speak on a regular basis she hadn't heard anything about the contents of my book. The result was she was able to pinpoint right away where my story got off track.

The bottom line here is that I am a big fan of early readers groups, but make sure yours has the right personnel makeup, as you will write a better book with the help of each and every one of them.

·····

TIP
16
. . . . .

Editorial and Marketing

Learn to Speak Effectively about Your Book

Learning to speak effectively about your book is one of the most important tips I can share with you. It's also an area that most authors need to improve considerably.

· · · · ·

Authors spend so much time writing their book that when asked to explain it, they often begin with a pause, followed by "ummmm . . ." That's not good, because from a marketing perspective you are by far the best spokesperson (and salesperson) for your book. You need to be able to effectively communicate your ideas and story line verbally. Potential readers get excited at the prospect of listening to an author speak, and doing so effectively can hook your listener, and hopefully entice them to buy and read your book!

Specifically, I recommend you prepare to be able to talk about your book in three different situations:

- **A one-minute blurb.** This is your elevator pitch (so named in the industry because you should be able to present it in the short time it takes to ride an elevator from one floor to the next). This sixty-second pitch answers the following questions: What is the title? What is the main idea or story line of your book? And what will readers get out of it? Why are you qualified to write this book? If you completed the exercises in Tips #8 and #9, this should be very easy.

- **A five- to ten-minute overview.** For nonfiction, in addition to the points in the one-minute blurb, what are the pillars that support your main idea? For fiction, give us a more in-depth look at your plot and characters. In either case, provide your listener with specific, compelling examples, and perhaps one anecdote about what makes your book unique.

- **A one-hour presentation.** This format is suitable for a radio interview or group presentation and includes all of the above but with more detail. For nonfiction, be sure to organize your ideas clearly, and support them with anecdotes whenever possible. For fiction, you will really need to address some of the themes of your book in addition to providing an enticing look into the plot and main characters.

In all cases, the key here is *practice.* The more you talk about your book and ideas, the better at it you will become. This is something that all experienced authors learn to do.

Every conversation you have about your book is an opportunity to generate some interest in your topic or plot, as well as build your platform. Each time you talk about your book with someone new, try ending the discussion with: "If you give me your email address, I'll be happy to send you an announcement when my book comes out." Or if your book is already out, say "Give me your email address and I will send you a link to my webpage with a full description of the book." If it takes you a year to write your book, think how many additional emails you will have by the time your book comes out.

Another benefit many authors don't realize at first is that talking about your book actually makes you a better writer! Here's why: Talking about your book can help you hone your ideas or story line. As you explain your points or tale to your listeners, you may actually hear yourself saying things about your topic or narrative that you realize should be in your manuscript.

When you talk to people about your book, you can watch their reactions and see where they become intrigued, bored, or lost. This will give you a clue about which areas to focus on and expand in your writing, as well as what you need to do a better job of explaining, or perhaps leave out altogether.

Some new authors are surprised by how much I stress the importance of speaking effectively about your book, but this is a vital skill that you will want to develop if you're going to reach a wide audience. Not only can it help you develop your ideas or storyline, but it will also help create a buzz about your book, build your platform, and prompt people to buy it!

* * * * *

Editorial

The Role of a Book Editor, and Why You Need One

As my friend Caroline Pincus, associate publisher at Conari Press, likes to say, "A good editor makes you sound like the best possible you that you can be."

Agood editor does not change your voice, but rather sharpens it. They also take into account the other tips I mention in this book during the editing process: helping you revise your work for the sake of clarity, focusing your book to stay on topic, and positioning your writing to appeal to your target audience.

Your editor not only helps make your prose be as clear as possible, but they also help you craft your message with the goal of reaching the widest possible audience. This additional element of thinking about the marketing of the book during the editing process, including your unique angle or "hook," is what separates a good book editor from a great book editor.

This is why it is best to work with an experienced book editor who is familiar with your genre, as he or she should know the other popular books on the market and be able to help you accentuate the ways in which your book is unique.

Some of the best-selling books I have published looked very different at press time from when the manuscript first arrived on my desk. The difference maker was the editor.

The key ingredient every author needs when it comes to working with a professional editor is willingness. You must be willing to listen and accept direction! In many cases, you are unable to see where your manuscript needs improvement, primarily because you are too close to it. As I mentioned in the introduction, many first-time authors have the art and inspiration, but they need to learn the craft of writing. This is where a great editor can really help.

If you plan to submit your manuscript to a traditional publisher, I suggest you work with an editor to get your manuscript or sample chapters in the best shape possible prior to submission. This may be the opposite of what some of you have heard, as authors often tell me, "I thought my publisher will have the book edited if they want to publish it."

That is true, the publisher may very well have your book edited. However, I think you have a better chance of being accepted by a traditional publisher if your manuscript has already been professionally edited (because if edited properly, your manuscript should be in great shape and have more appeal to the potential publisher!). At the very least, I would suggest a professional edit of the sample chapters you are submitting with your proposal. Even if you cannot find a traditional publisher to take on your book, your manuscript is now edited and you are ready to self-publish.

Lastly, a note of caution. Some authors go the other way, and expect their editor to do more than is customary. Do not expect your editor to write your book or sections of your book for you. If that is what you are looking for, then you want a ghostwriter or a coauthor. We'll cover the difference between those two in Tip #25.

⚬ ⚬ ⚬ ⚬ ⚬

Editorial

Drown Your Darlings

Almost every writer has the tendency to include things in his or her manuscript that they feel are important but that do not necessarily serve the overall purpose of the book. These add-ons are called your "author darlings," and you must get rid of them. An objective early reader can help you identify these spots, but if they get past this person your editor will certainly find them.

•••••

For nonfiction authors, look at your manuscript and see where you go off on a tangent. Where are you trying to say too much? Sometimes a nonfiction author will spend pages explaining a detailed nuance of their subject matter when a much simpler explanation will do. Or you may have allowed yourself to go off topic because you think this additional information is "so interesting," assuming that your reader will as well. And let me remind you again about the dangers of including too much of your personal experience in a book, because doing so can be interpreted as self-serving by your reader.

And for my fiction authors, while I don't know who originally coined the phrase "drown your darlings," it's pretty clear it was done with you in mind! As a fiction author myself, I cut more than 10,000 words from a 70,000 word manuscript under the direction of my editor, and it was all my darlings! While it was difficult for me to do that, these parts were slowing down the pace of my novel by taking the characters to places they didn't need to go. My challenge to you is to look at your manuscript with this in mind. Remember your overall plot and story line. Where do you stray from it? If you do stray, there had better be a darn good reason, and usually there isn't.

In summary, author darlings are the parts in your book that are important to you but detract from the overall message or story line. You must identify and remove them to keep your readers engaged and give your book the best possible chance to reach a wide audience.

•••••

TIP

19
•••••

Marketing

Speak Directly to Your Potential Readers

Even in the high-tech information age of social media, nothing sells a book better than a face-to-face encounter with the author. Absolutely nothing. As a result, I tell every author I know to conduct as many lectures and workshops on their book as they possibly can.

For nonfiction authors, since you are presenting yourself as an expert in a particular field, your job is to find and gather those people who are interested in learning about your topic and ideas. One resource for doing this is www.meetup.com. Organized by interest, meetup.com has created a virtual meeting place for people interested in everything from sailing to Transcendental Meditation to connect and then set up face-to-face group meetup. This is a wonderful resource for authors to either start their own meetup.com group or reach out to other meetup groups in their area of expertise and offer to present at their next gathering. My experience is that many existing meetup groups welcome expert guest presenters.

For fiction authors, it can be more difficult to gather people and talk about your story line, characters, etc., but that shouldn't dissuade you from trying to do so when the opportunity arises. Meetup.com offers other sources for fiction authors such as writing groups and book club discussion groups. While some writing groups and book club discussion groups focus on both nonfiction and fiction alike, many of the these groups focus on fiction only. Participating in a writers group will give you a chance to get your writing reviewed for free. And since most writers of fiction are also readers of fiction, in addition to gaining some insights on becoming a better writer, you are also creating a future readership base (a.k.a. building your platform!).

Once your book is out, book clubs can be a wonderful resource for fiction authors. I suggest contacting book clubs and offering to meet with them for a discussion or presentation after their members have had a chance to read your book.

For nonfiction and fiction alike, I also encourage you to conduct free conference calls and teleclasses to discuss your ideas and book with potential readers. Websites like www.freeconferencing.com provide the technology to host and record these calls at no cost to you. This allows you to connect with people all over the globe and talk about your ideas and story line. Here is another place social media can really be useful, as many authors invite those who are following them on social media to join them in a free call.

Almost every author I publish is required to conduct a three- to four-week teleclass on the topics covered in their book, with the only admission price being that the attendees must purchase the book. This provides readers a chance to speak directly with an author, and it's an effective way to get sales started.

Connecting with your readers, either face-to-face or via telephone, also gives you the opportunity to create something else: a fan for life. Readers who have a direct encounter with an author and like their current book are much more likely to buy the author's next book when it comes out.

EXERCISE

Transcribe your lectures and workshops, or read your manuscript aloud.

Once you have begun to give lectures or conduct conference calls, make sure you record them and then play them back, transcribing as you go along.

For nonfiction authors, these recordings can be an excellent source of material for your book. They will also help you talk about your book more effectively. Something happens when we listen to ourselves explain our main ideas, as the way we say something spontaneously can sometimes be better than all our intentional craftiness behind a computer.

Some best-selling nonfiction books are actually modified transcriptions of verbal presentations, such as the now-famous book *The Last Lecture* by Randy Pausch. Another book that was not-so-famous but was still very successful is *Awareness: The Perils and Opportunities of Reality,* by Jesuit priest Anthony De Mello. It is adapted from a workshop the author presented and has gone on to sell hundreds of thousands of copies.

Recording and transcribing your lectures can also be a great jump-start when dealing with writer's block. By having your presentation material down on the page, you can edit, rearrange, and get your writing moving again.

Finally, this exercise will help your marketing efforts by making you a better presenter of your topic, as you are now "in the audience" and can listen for ways to refine and clarify your message.

While fiction authors can also benefit from transcriptions of their lectures, I suggest another similar exercise that is more appropriate for your genre. Go to a quiet room and read your book out loud. Parts of it may sound very different from what you had imagined. This exercise can show you where things get choppy or don't read well, especially when the passage includes dialogue and description.

●　●　●　●　●

TIP

20

• • • • •

Editorial

Find the Right Editor for You

I know it can be difficult for unpublished
authors to connect with good book editors,
so this tip will be devoted to ways in which
you can find one.

O nce you have been to the bookstore and determined your book's category (see the exercise in Tip #5), look at the author acknowledgments in the best-selling books in that same category. Oftentimes the author will thank his or her editor, and this may be a potential editor for you too. Do a web search on that person's name and the words "book editor" together (for example, "John Smith book editor") and see if a website or contact information comes up. Many editors are freelancers, and if you can convince them to take on your project, you know you are working with an experienced book editor who is also familiar with your genre.

If the authors of the most popular books in your genre have not thanked their editors in the acknowledgments, consider doing a web search of the titles of these books followed by the words "book editor" (for example, "*East of Eden* book editor"). Freelance editors often list the books they have edited on their websites as well, so you may find the editor of the book that way.

Another step would be to use the various publishing guides available in bookstores and online. This will require some discernment on your part. If you go this route, be prepared to ask your potential editor for a list of books that he or she has edited. Hopefully these are books you have read or are at least familiar with, and if not, go read some of them before making a decision.

Once you have made contact with an editor and are considering hiring them, you need to see a sample of what they can do (and a good editor needs to see a sample of what you can do), before you both decide if it's a good fit. This can be done by providing a sample chapter or two to the editor and paying a small critique fee ($100 or $200 generally). The editor should then provide you a one-page assessment of your strengths and weaknesses, a description of how they can help you, and a quote for what their services cost. Remember that the good editors can be expensive, as they are being paid for their time and there are only so many hours in a workweek. Sometimes authors think editors should provide a free assessment and quote for their services, and I couldn't disagree more. Once you have found an experienced, well-qualified editor, you should show them you're serious about your writing by paying them a modest assessment fee.

These are just a few suggestions for finding the right editor for you. Writers' groups and university classes can provide some other options. But I strongly encourage you to use a professional book editor, not a friend or someone from your early readers group. A good book editor is someone who has the proven skills and successful track record to help you get your book into the best shape possible!

* * * * *

Business

What Makes a Book a "Best Seller"?

I often begin my author workshops with this question: How many copies does a book need to sell in the first year before it is considered "successful" by a traditional publisher? The answers I receive usually range between 50,000 and 100,000 copies, sometimes all the way up to a million copies. But for the vast, vast majority of books published, none of these answers are even close.

．．．．．

While sales expectations can differ widely depending on the book and who publishes it, in general most authors are surprised to learn that a small to medium-size publisher generally considers a book successful if it sells between 3,000 and 5,000 copies in the first year.

Now, the larger the publishing house, the higher the sales expectations are for a book. In part that's because they have higher costs that must be factored into each title they print (employee salaries, rent, other overhead costs, etc.), as well as higher profit expectations. But speaking for my publishing company and many others of similar size, selling 3,000 to 5,000 copies in the first year is the minimum benchmark. And while many of our books sell far more than this, for a book written by a first-time author, these are acceptable numbers.

I share this information with you so that when you set your sales goals for your first book you can keep these numbers in mind. This is usually a surprise to most new authors, but remember that the books you hear most about are the ones that sell millions and millions of copies. These titles—the Harry Potters, the Twilights, and the Da Vinci Codes—represent a very tiny fraction of all books published.

Turning to self-published books, I have read that the average number of copies sold in the United States is between 100 and 200 per book, and most of these purchases come from the author's friends and family. Now remember, this takes into account all self-published books, where all the author typically does is write his or her manuscript without any direction or guidance, self-publishes the book, and lists it for sale on Amazon. Now you can see why platform, editing, and the other tips in this book are so important, because without implementing these strategies, sales likely fall into this range.

Despite this, it appears that more and more authors, especially self-published ones, are claiming "best seller" status for their books. What do they mean by that? "Best seller" where? For example, if a book sells twenty-five copies at the local convenience store in your small town, and the next top-selling book at that store sells twenty-four copies, I guess one could say that at this particular store the first book was a best seller. While this is an exaggerated example, the point I want to make is that when you hear an author bestow the title "best seller" on his or her book, it may be worth inquiring into how they arrived at that conclusion.

In the publishing world, the gold standard for declaring a book a best seller is the *New York Times* Best Seller list. Each week this well-respected newspaper prints a list of the best-selling books in the country, classified by category. The editors at the *Times* have a very secretive process for determining which books make this list, but I do know it involves receiving sales data from a variety of national booksellers in order to determine how many books were bought by customers the previous week. In addition, there is not a set number of copies you need to sell in one week to make the list, because the best sellers are picked in relation to what other books are selling that week.

That being said, I can say with a good degree of confidence that if your book sells 25,000 copies in one week through the largest retailers in the United States, it will most likely make the *New York Times* Best Seller list.

So when an author says, "My book was a *New York Times* best seller," you can be sure this means far more than an author who uses sales figures from their local convenience store to make a best seller claim.

In summary, the designation "best seller" largely depends on the publishing house. For a small to medium-size publisher, a best seller may be a book that sells 20,000 copies in the first year, while at a larger publishing house, that figure may be significantly higher.

A final word about sales and best seller claims: Almost every traditional publisher subscribes to a service called Nielsen BookScan, which gives us sales data from all the major booksellers. And while small bookstores and author direct sales don't appear in BookScan's totals, this service gives traditional publishers a pretty good idea of how many copies a book has actually sold.

I mention this as a word of caution to self-published authors who want to exaggerate their sales data when submitting their self-published book to a traditional publisher. The publisher has a quick and easy way to verify your claims via this service. Nothing kills a book proposal faster than an author who claims his or her book has sold 5,000 copies, while BookScan shows it as selling only 150.

• • • • •

Note: Amazon gives authors access to their BookScan numbers via its Author Central service. So once your book is published (either through a traditional publisher or self-publishing), make sure you register for this free service. Besides gaining access to your sales data, you'll also want to sign up and update your Author Central profile as a matter of marketing and platform building, as this is the information readers see in the About the Author section of the book sales page on Amazon.

• • • • •

Business

The Return of the Brick-and-Mortar Bookstore and the Distribution Model

Based on the title of this tip, you may have presumed I was going to write about the resurgence in the number of physical retail bookstores. Sadly, this is not the case. The "return" I am speaking of here is one of the most difficult hurdles facing publishers and authors alike.

The Bookselling Business Model

Imagine walking into Macy's, or any other retail clothing store, and every product for sale was returnable to the manufacturer for a full refund if it didn't sell, and that return policy was good forever. You can imagine how a business model like that would turn the retail clothing world upside down.

And yet, this is exactly the way the book business works. Bookstores may return books to the publishers for a full refund at any time, even years after they first ordered the book![2] As you can see, this business model greatly increases the risk exposure by the publisher and has negative consequences for authors as well.

The reasoning behind this odd retail model needs further explanation. The bookstore's position is that if the return policy were not in place, they would have to become "experts" on every genre and category and would be extremely picky about what books they carried on their shelves. Instead, they look to traditional publishers to vet the author's writing and only publish those authors with the best and brightest ideas.

The bookstore further reasons that if a reputable publisher is willing to invest all the necessary money it takes to create and promote a book, then the publisher must feel it will sell, and the store is willing to carry it on its shelves. But if the book doesn't sell, the store will quickly send it back for a refund.

---

[2] The only exception to this is when a book is declared "out of print" by a publisher. In this case, the publisher must give the bookstores a six-month warning so they can return any copies they have on hand if they choose to. (Most of them do.)

This open-ended return policy forces a traditional publisher to think long and hard before publishing any given book. It is also a main reason why it is so difficult for self-published books to break into mainstream bookstores. With a traditional publisher, not only is it presumed that the book has been vetted by the publisher, but the bookstore knows that they can return the book for a refund, as they have a longstanding financial relationship with the publisher.

With a self-published author, the bookstore does not have the confidence that they can return the books so easily for a refund, so generally a self-published book has to be selling quite strongly before a bookstore will be interested in carrying it.

Distribution

Now let's talk about distribution. The word "distribution" refers to the process of how a book gets from the publisher to the world at large.

Traditional book publishers have accounts with all the major bookstores, online booksellers, and book wholesalers,[3] so the corporate buyers at these organizations can place orders from the publisher with ease. In addition, traditional publishers employ sales reps for their titles (called book reps), who meet with bookstore buyers on a regular basis and "pitch" them on the publisher's upcoming books.

Most self-published books do not have a distribution method beyond the book being available on Amazon and other e-tailer sites. Virtually any self-published author can create an account on Amazon and similar sites to sell their self-published book, and most self-publishing companies include this service for authors.

---

[3] Book wholesalers serve as a middleman between publisher and bookstore, allowing smaller bookstores to order from one place rather than placing orders with several different publishers.

So as you can see, the distribution infrastructure established long ago by traditional publishers and booksellers provides a tremendous benefit for traditionally published authors. It means their book is far more likely to be in bookstores.

However, I hope you remember from the opening tip in this book, just getting your book into the bookstore is not the guaranteed path to success it once was. Years ago, when readers' only place to buy books was from a bookstore, getting your book into the bookstore was essential for success. Now, as so many people research and buy books online, getting into the bookstore isn't as important as it once was, and platform and author marketing have become more important now than ever before.

· · · · ·

Business

Parlez-Vous Français?

A significant source of revenue for traditional publishers and many of their authors comes from foreign translation rights.

•••••

Almost every widely spoken language in the world represents a translation opportunity for a book. Because most first-time author contracts with a traditional publisher include "world rights" to publish the book, if a foreign publisher wants to publish your book in the native language of their country they must purchase the rights to do so from the U.S. publisher. The publisher then shares the revenue of that purchase with you.

You see this regularly on the covers of best-selling books, where it may state something like "translated into thirty-five languages."

This is the normal way the publishing world works, as otherwise your U.S. publisher would have to translate, print, and sell a book directly in other countries, and comply with all the laws of that land. It is far easier and more effective to simply sell the rights to publish the book in a particular country to a well-established publisher in said country. If you are a first-time author, you can typically expect to split the proceeds from these foreign translation rights sales with your publisher fifty-fifty.

Next to getting distribution in the mainstream bookstores this is one of the biggest benefits of going with a traditional publisher. Traditional publishers either have an experienced foreign rights department or an outside foreign rights agent who is in regular contact with publishers around the world. In addition, foreign publishers have the benefit of buying and translating a book that has already been professionally edited and in most cases has demonstrated a successful sales track record in the United States.

It is very, very difficult for a self-published author to get noticed by foreign publishers, even if their book is selling well in U.S. markets. Generally, authors don't know which publishers to contact in other countries, and like bookstores, the foreign publishers prefer to deal with traditional publishing companies. Consequently, access to foreign markets is one of the biggest reasons why successful self-published authors ultimately sign with a traditional publisher.

Technically speaking, foreign translation rights fall under the larger umbrella of subsidiary rights in author-publisher contracts. Other subsidiary rights that can be sold include things like the audio rights to your book, excerpts from your book for other publications (called serial rights), products, and even movie or television deals.

With the exception of having your book made into an audio book, most other subsidiary rights don't come into play unless your book becomes a mega-seller, but they should always be addressed in your contract with a traditional publisher.

FUN FACT

It is far more common for a book first published in the United States to be translated into other languages than for a book to be published in another country first and then come to the United States. A notable exception to this trend is *The Alchemist,* one of the best-selling novels of all time, which was originally written in Portuguese and published by a small house in Brazil.

• • • • •

Business

Understanding the Role of a Literary Agent

I am often asked in my author workshops questions such as:

What exactly does a literary agent do?

As a first-time author, do I need an agent to get published?

How do I find an agent?

et's address those questions here, one at a time. First, a literary agent is someone who will represent you and your book to prospective publishers. A good agent can help you by providing editorial guidance on your manuscript and proposal, matching your work with an appropriate publishing house, handling contract negotiations, and being a wonderful resource to explain and guide you through the process of creating a successful book in general. For their services, agents typically earn 12–15 percent of the royalties (including the advance) you receive from a publisher.

Now, to answer the question of whether or not you *need* a literary agent is more complex. Let's begin with the current hierarchy in the world of traditional publishers. Quite frankly, it is a case where size matters. The bigger the publishing house you want to approach, the more likely you will need an agent to get to them.

To make this explanation simple, I will classify all traditional publishers in either one of two camps. The first camp is comprised of the big New York houses, publishers such as Penguin Random House, HarperCollins, Simon & Schuster, and the like. With few exceptions, the big houses will not accept un-agented submissions. So if you plan to submit to one of the largest publishing houses in America, the answer is generally "Yes! You need an agent." The second camp of traditional publishers is easy to classify: it's every publisher that is not in the first camp. This is a wide range of small to medium-size publishers, many of which are multimillion dollar companies, and the majority of them will accept proposals from authors directly, without an agent. This doesn't mean that small to mid-size publishers won't accept agented submissions—they certainly will, and some prefer it. But the point I want to make is that you do not need an agent to get a book deal from many of these smaller publishers.

Keep in mind that a very tiny percentage of books published by the big New York houses are from first-time authors. Instead, the vast majority of first-time authors are published by small to mid-size publishers. So do you *need* an agent? Only if you are to be published in the least likely of places.

That being said, an agent can still provide you with a valuable service, especially in the areas of education and preparation. However, because many first-time authors have difficulty finding an agent, I want to be clear that you do not need one to be published by the majority of traditional publishers.

Speaking for my own company, I can tell you that we treat every submission equally, regardless of whether or not an author is represented by an agent. Also, our publishing contract for first-time authors is the same regardless of whether you have an agent or not.

If you've determined that you do want an agent, there are a few ways to go about finding one. There are various writers conferences held around the country each year, and many of these give you an opportunity to meet with agents face-to-face. I recommend doing a web search on "author conferences" to find some that are close to you.

And as I mentioned in Tip #20 about finding an editor, many authors will thank their agent in the acknowledgments section of their book. You can search for that agent's name online to find out how to get in touch.

In addition, a handful of reference books are published each year that list agents, editors, publishers, and the like, and while these resources are a little less personal, they can still provide some good leads. Agents tend to specialize in particular genres or categories, so if you choose to work with one, make sure they have experience in yours.

The bottom line on agents is that they can definitely be of benefit to you as an author, especially if you can find one with whom you can develop a good working relationship. That being said, do not be discouraged or dissuaded from pursuing your publishing goals if you are unable to find an agent to work with, as you can succeed without one.

●●●●●

TIP
25
• • • • •

Editorial, Marketing, and Business

The Benefits of a Coauthor (and What Is a Ghost?)

I have a dear friend who is one of the most published authors in existence. But by her own admission, she is simply not a good writer, and she has no desire to improve in this area. Despite that, her books have sold millions of copies and have received hundreds upon hundreds of positive reviews.

How is that possible, you ask? Enter her coauthor.

By definition, a coauthor is someone whose name will appear with yours on the cover of the book. This type of relationship is often the case when you see a book cover that states "Author A" in large letters, and just under that "with Author B" appears in much smaller type. A coauthor will share with you in the work, the recognition, and the royalties. Depending on the situation, they may even be the lead writer of the book.

This typically occurs in a nonfiction book where one author may have the necessary knowledge or expert experience in a particular subject, but they are not a strong writer, or perhaps they don't have the time or they prefer not to write. This author may take on a coauthor with the purpose of improving the prose of the manuscript. This was certainly the case with my friend. She has a wonderful platform and is well known in her area of expertise. She was highly sought after by publishers to "write a book," but she didn't care much for the writing process. She began working with a seasoned coauthor, and together they have produced more than one *New York Times* best seller. This is only one example for coauthorship. In many cases, two authors who both enjoy the writing process have chosen to work together because each author brings an equal share of knowledge and experience to the book. This is very common too, and often the authors' names will be the same size on the book and appear in alphabetical order.

Coauthorship also occurs in fiction, albeit not as much.

A ghostwriter, on the other hand, is exactly what the name implies—a ghost. They are writing the book for you and giving you all the credit. Typically this is done for a flat fee up front, and they do not share in the royalties.

Some fiction and memoir authors have teamed up with a ghostwriter when they felt they had an incredible story to tell, but for whatever reason they did not want to write the book, or they felt it would be better served by having a seasoned writer at the keyboard. I am not going to say much more about ghostwriters, because if you are reading this book you are probably not using one. But it is important for you to know the difference between a coauthor and ghost.

• • • • •

Business

Traditional Publishing versus Self-Publishing: The Major Differences Explained

While I realize that many reading this want to be published by a traditional publisher, the facts are that some of you will ultimately go the self-publishing route. In my opinion, this can be an excellent road to take. Let's not forget that some of the most successful authors in the business originally published their work themselves: Ken Blanchard (*The One-Minute Manager*), James Redfield (*The Celestine Prophecy*), Richard Nelson Bolles (*What Color Is Your Parachute?*), and more recently, E. L. James (*Fifty Shades of Grey*).

• • • • •

In addition, self-publishing has some clear advantages over traditional publishing, at least initially. A couple of the major benefits of self-publishing are total control and the potential for earning more if your book sells well.

Total Control

When you choose to self-publish, you have the final say over the title, cover, and most importantly, the content of your book. All final decisions about the book are yours, and yours alone. Not so with traditional publishing!

If you sign with a publishing house, the publisher, who is investing the money, will have the final say on the cover and title for sure, and in some cases they will only agree to publish a book after you have made any content changes the publisher deems necessary. Now, I would like to add that in most cases the changes the publisher wants to make to a book are probably the right ones, and every publisher I know strives to come to an agreement with an author that is satisfactory to both parties. But when this can't be done, self-publishing frees the author from any type of editorial conformity or compromise.

More Risk but Also More Reward

One of the primary reasons a book is turned down by a traditional house is that the publisher does not feel the book is commercially viable. In other words, they don't think they will sell enough copies to make it worth their investment. The publisher may think a book is well written, and they may like many of the author's ideas, but the business of publishing requires factoring in a profit and loss forecast, and some books are rejected for this reason alone. Self-publishing gives the author a chance to prove the publisher wrong! Since you are taking the financial risk when self-publishing, it only makes sense that you can earn more if things go well, especially in the beginning. We'll discuss this more in the next tip, but your "royalty rate," or the amount you receive as the author when your book sells through Amazon or other e-tailers, should be substantially more than if you were to go with a traditional publisher. Remember, you have paid the upfront costs of producing your book, not someone else, so you will reap the financial rewards if sales are strong.

A sequence of events that I am seeing more and more in the industry is that self-published books that enjoy some initial success are often picked up by a traditional house in order to help sales get to the next level by getting the book into mainstream bookstores across the country, and ultimately around the world via their relationships with foreign publishers.

If you remember Tips #22 and #23, two of the biggest things traditional publishers bring to the table are (1) bookstore distribution and (2) foreign rights translation revenue. If a self-published author later signs with a traditional publisher, it will mean giving up a share of the profits on a per book basis, but the author will almost assuredly make up that amount in quantity of books sold and royalties from foreign translation sales.

Overall, I want to leave you with the understanding that self-publishing has some clear advantages, especially initially, that you don't have if you go with a traditional publisher. And for many notable author names, self-publishing was the first step on their road to success.

· · · · ·

Business

A Financial Litmus Test for Comparing Self-Publishing Companies

As mentioned in the previous tip, self-publishing is a great option for many authors. And with so many companies out there who want to help you self-publish your book, how is an author to know which one to choose? Well, that is the purpose of this tip, because there are three vital items you should evaluate when comparing self-publishing companies:

What is the upfront fee to produce your book, and what do you receive for this fee?

What is your royalty rate on books sold through the retail channels?

What is your author discount when it comes to purchasing your own books?

What Will It Cost to Produce Your Book?

This is the obvious first step when comparing a list of quality self-publishing companies. But you want to be very clear not only on the upfront fee of producing your book, but also on what is included for that fee. For instance, do you get multiple cover concepts to choose from before deciding on a final for your book? If so, how many? Does the fee include copy editing and proofreading of your manuscript? How many paperback books will be included in the fee, if any? Will they offer professional guidance along the way? Will they produce an e-book as well? Do they list your book for sale on Amazon and other e-tailers? Most companies will provide a listing of all the benefits you receive in an upfront package, so be sure to make a chart with the answers to each of these questions for every company you're considering for comparison.

Cost is the easiest criterion of the three to evaluate, and unfortunately it's oftentimes the *only* one that some authors look at when choosing a self-publishing company. As you will see after reading the next two criteria, the upfront fee doesn't tell the whole story.

How Much Will You Make on Each Copy Sold?

When your book sells on Amazon.com, BN.com, another e-tailer's website, or the self-publishing company's website, what percentage of that sale will you receive?

Here's where things start to get murky, as I have seen self-publishing companies manipulate the language here to make it sound like you're getting an incredible deal, when in fact you may not be. For instance, I've seen advertisements like this before:

OUR AUTHORS RECEIVE 100 PERCENT OF THE ROYALTIES (AFTER EXPENSES)

This raises the question, what do they count as "expenses"? Other advertisements I have seen say things like, "We offer a 50 percent royalty rate minus production costs." Here again, what do they include in "production costs"? Because the royalty rate can be easily manipulated with this type of language, I recommend you ask each of the self-publishing companies you are considering the following question: If my book is 216 pages, has a cover price of $20, and a copy sells on Amazon, how much money will I receive from the sale of that one book?

Now we can compare apples to apples. With the page count and cover price, they should be able to give you a pretty accurate answer of how much money you would receive per sale. Now you have a figure you can actually compare between self-publishing companies to see how much you can earn on the back end. For instance, if in answer to that question Company A says you will receive 100 percent of net after expenses, and that amounts to $1 per book, and Company B says you will receive only a 30 percent net royalty but that comes out to $3 per book, it's easy to see that in this case, a royalty rate of 30 percent with Company B is better than a royalty rate of 100 percent with Company A.

What Is Your Author Discount?

This is an incredibly vital component to evaluate when choosing a company to assist you with self-publishing, and unfortunately it is also the item that most authors fail to even consider.

If you've learned anything from the previous tips about platform building, as well as first generation and second generation sales, you know that the best spokesperson and salesperson for your book is you! As a result, the majority of initial sales will come from you. You want to be out there selling as many books as possible for two reasons: (1) If your author discount is good, then this is the quickest and surest way for you to recoup your initial investment, and (2) selling your book directly is the best thing you can do to help your book take off and begin to sell on its own.

Because of the importance and necessity of selling your book directly, I strongly recommend working with a self-publishing company that offers you a discount of at least 50 percent off the cover price when you purchase your own book. (But remember, author purchases are royalty exclusive, so you won't be paid a royalty on books you purchase yourself.) Sadly, I see many self-publishing companies offering discounts far lower than this, with some offering no discount at all!

Let's take Company A again, the one that promised you a low upfront fee and 100 percent of royalties after expenses. Imagine you could only buy books for 15 percent off the cover price. That means if your book has a cover price of $20, you would purchase it for $17. Assuming you sold it at your own lecture or other direct means, you could make $3 per book.

Company B offers you an author discount of 50 percent off the cover price. That means your $20 book now costs you $10, and for every copy of your book you sell on your own you profit $10. Now you can really make up some ground quickly.

• • • • •

Now let's look at a true comparison of Company A and Company B, taking into account the answers to these three questions.

	Company A	Company B
Upfront Cost	$1,000	$2,000
Royalty Rate (based on $20 cover price, sold on Amazon.com)	100% = $1 per book	30% = $3 per book
Author Purchase Discount	15%	50%

If you sell 100 copies through Amazon and 300 copies directly through events, here is the complete financial picture:

	Company A	Company B
Royalties Paid Out through Self-Publishing Company	$100 (100 books at $1 per book)	$300 (100 books at $3 per book)
Profit Earned from Author Direct Sales	$900 (300 books at $3 profit per book)	$3,000 (300 books at $10 profit per book)
Subtotal of Earnings	$1,000	$3,300
Less Your Initial Investment	($1,000)	($2,000)
True Profit	$0	$1,300

You can see that the lowest upfront price doesn't always translate into the best long-term financial deal. Of course it may, but that is only if your book doesn't sell, and who wants that?

Retain Your Rights

One final note of extreme importance before signing a contract with a self-publishing company: make sure that you retain full rights to your book. You paid for the production, you should have the right to "take it back" anytime you want. This is important, because if your book is successful and you are approached by a traditional publisher down the line, you want to be able to cancel your contract with the self-publishing company without any penalty.

While this is the normal course of business for most self-publishing companies, occasionally I come across a self-publishing company that won't let the author cancel the agreement without the consent of the company. This gives them a license to hold the author hostage if the book takes off.

I met an author once whose self-published book was selling very well. I invited him to join the Hierophant family, which he was eager to do, only to learn when he went to cancel his contract with the self-publishing company that they wanted a hefty fee for cancelation. This was an unfortunate situation for the author, as he had paid this company several thousand dollars up front to publish his book.

All of this can be avoided by confirming that you retain the rights to your book, and you may notify the company to cease the publication and sale of it at any time. You won't receive a refund for the upfront fees you paid for production, and there is generally a provision that allows them to sell any remaining copies of the book they have in stock, but neither of these things will be important if a greater opportunity for you and your book presents itself.

● ● ● ● ●

Business

Royalty Rates and Advances in Traditional Publishing

Royalties

Before jumping into a discussion of royalty rates, I need to explain the two primary ways royalties are calculated in the traditional publishing world: as a percentage of "gross receipts" or a percentage of "net receipts."

The gross receipts calculation method means that the royalty rate will be determined on the book's cover price. The net receipts royalty method means that the royalty rate will be calculated according to the amount the publisher actually receives for the book.

If you remember from our discussion about distribution, the publisher sets the cover price for the book and sells the book to bookstores for about 50 percent off the cover price (the discount can be slightly more or less, but a rule of thumb is 50 percent). When a publisher uses the net royalty calculation, they are referring to cover price less this discount, or the net amount the publisher receives for the sale from the bookstore or book wholesaler.

For example, if your book had a cover price of $20, a royalty rate of 10 percent of gross is roughly equivalent to a rate of 20 percent of net. See the table below for the math on this.

	Gross Method	Net Method
Cover Price (Gross)	$20	$20
Amount Received by Publisher (Net)	$10	$10
Royalty Rate	10% of gross	20% of net
Royalty Earned	$2	$2

When presented with a contract from a traditional publisher, it's important to pay attention to whether they are using the *gross* method or *net* method when paying royalties, as 10 percent of gross would be a generous offer, but 10 percent of net would not be.

While rates at different publishing houses will vary by a few percentage points, in general first-time authors who sign with a small to mid-size publishing firm can expect royalty rates between 5–7.5 percent of gross, or 10–15 percent of net. The largest publishing houses typically pay rates that are a little higher than these.

Most publishing houses pay royalties every six months. You as an author receive a statement showing the number of books sold and any foreign translation or other subsidiary rights revenue. Your final payment for the period should be the sum of those two less a "reserve for returns," generally 20–30 percent of the number of books sold. You should remember the reason for this reserve from the tip explaining bookstore returns, as publishers want to protect themselves should your book be returned by the bookstore instead of being sold to a reader.

Advances

Now for a discussion of book advances. An advance is the amount of money a publisher pays you prior to publication (or sometimes coinciding with publication) of your book. It is an "advance" against future royalties, meaning that if you receive an advance of $2,000, and your royalty amount is $2 per book, you will not receive a royalty payment on book sales until after the first 1,000 copies are sold.

From a publisher's point of view, the advance amount often depends on how "risky" the book is from a profitability standpoint. When determining what advance to offer an author, a traditional publisher may estimate the minimum number of copies they expect the book to sell in the first year. They may also add in any amounts expected from the sale of foreign rights translations or other subsidiary rights, giving them a rough estimate of what the author would receive over the course of the first year. The advance offered will generally match this figure.

Advance amounts for first-time authors with small to medium-size publishing houses often range between $1,000 and $3,000, and in special cases can go as high as $10,000. If a book is very risky the publisher may offer no advance. For established authors, especially those at large publishing houses, the advance amounts can be much higher.

Once your book earns more in royalties than the advance amount, then your book has "earned out," which is a good thing in the publishing world, as it indicates your publisher has received the return on their advance investment and you can expect royalty checks going forward. Authors at small and medium publishing firms whose books do not earn out are far less likely to receive an offer to have their next book published.

As a first-time author, if you are offered a deal from a traditional publishing house, I wouldn't be overly concerned about the advance amount. Remember, it's simply an advance against future royalties, so if you go out and promote your book effectively and it takes off, you should earn well beyond the amount of your advance.

• • • • •

Marketing Your Book via TV, Radio, and Print/Digital Media

We've already covered some of the ways you can use the Internet and social media to spread awareness about your book and ideas. In this tip, let's examine the traditional channels of public relations: TV, radio, and print (including specialty websites and online magazines).

• • • • •

I want to begin by stating that for the vast majority of first-time authors, social media websites, as well as lectures, workshops, and the like, are the most effective ways to build your platform and create awareness for you and your book. However, you don't want to ignore the traditional channels of TV, radio, and print (including online magazines and other content-driven websites). Because most media in today's market is niche, you want to be very focused when reaching out to these outlets, and only go after those that are a good match for your topic and book. Also, having media coverage for yourself (and your book) with things like positive reviews, feature stories, and interviews will not only help sell your book, but it can also grow your platform and raise your overall notoriety as an author.

Radio

Of these traditional sources, radio is one of my favorites for first-time authors. You can do radio interviews via phone or Skype from your home, and if it's the right radio show, meaning it has a large audience and is a good fit for your book, it can really move some copies.

For example, *Coast to Coast AM,* hosted by George Noory, is broadcast nightly on radio stations around the country and focuses on topics like UFOs, after-death communication, ancient civilizations, and other unexplained phenomena. If you have written a book on one of these topics, getting interviewed on this radio show would be a home run hit! But if you've written a cookbook or romance novel, *Coast to Coast AM* would be a waste of your time (and theirs, so they likely wouldn't be interested in interviewing you!).

Since we are on the topic of radio, I would like to issue a word of caution here. The invention of Internet radio has made it inexpensive and easy to start and host shows from anywhere on the planet. Unfortunately, many of these shows have little or no audience and will not do much toward building your platform or selling books. (On the bright side, these shows can be a great place to learn how to give radio interviews with little downside if you perform poorly.)

In preparing to give radio interviews, remember that most shows expect you to provide them with a list of questions you want to be asked during the interview. This is good for both parties, as it allows the host to focus on the topics that you feel are the best, namely those that will get the audience most excited about you and your book.

Magazines and Niche Websites

Magazines and niche websites are the next area I like when it comes to traditional publicity options. Again, it's important here that the outlets be a good fit for you and your book, and if they are, you may be able to get your book reviewed by them, or they may even invite you to be a guest columnist.

In Hierophant Publishing's primary publishing genre, self-help/personal development, a good example of a niche website is www.vividlife.me, which carries the tagline "Daily Inspirations for Living Your Ultimate Life." As it suggests, this website features articles and book reviews by some of the best-selling self-help authors in the country. Getting featured here can give your book and platform a real boost! Finding the right magazines and websites that match your book's topic is key to getting meaningful coverage.

National Television

National TV is the most difficult medium for unknown authors to access, but overall I wouldn't be too concerned, as being on TV does not necessarily guarantee you will sell books. Of course, there is one very famous exception to this rule: Oprah Winfrey!

When it comes to books, her ability to create interest and sales is unmatched. For example, my publishing colleagues at Red Wheel/Weiser Books and Conari Press published a book in May of 2000 titled *The Book of Awakening: Having the Life You Want by Being Present to the Life You Have* by Mark Nepo. It is a wonderfully written self-help book that for its first ten years in print maintained solid, although not record-setting, sales (about 5,000 copies per year).

Then, in the fall of 2010, Oprah held up *The Book of Awakening* on her talk show and announced that it was one of her "ultimate favorite things." Over the next few weeks, the book made the *New York Times* Best Seller list and sold more copies in this short time period than it had in the ten years prior!

The Oprah effect is undeniable. However, if your marketing plan consists of sending your book to Oprah, be warned, I have heard through reliable sources that Oprah receives so many unsolicited books that neither she, nor her show producers, could possibly read all of them.[4]

Other than Oprah, there really aren't many defining TV personalities that are well known for selling books. I am not suggesting that going on TV with your book is a bad idea, it's wonderful if it happens, but I don't think making this a top priority makes sense for most authors.

---

[4] While Oprah no longer does a regular show on ABC, she currently interviews authors on her *Super Soul Sunday* show, *Oprah's Lifeclass*, and *Master Class*, all airing on her cable network, OWN.

Local Papers and TV

Your local newspapers and TV stations oftentimes have an interest in covering authors from the community. This can be a great way to get some free press coverage. You can also present yourself and your book to the morning and afternoon news programs at your local ABC, CBS, FOX, or NBC broadcast affiliates. If you live in a major media market like New York or Los Angeles this might be more difficult, but it is still worth a try. The only exception to this is the cable morning shows, as some of them charge you to be interviewed on the show, and the fees can be very expensive. I have never seen a situation where a show like this provided a worthwhile return on the investment.

• • • • •

Marketing and Business

The Role of a Contract Publicist or PR Firm

From a purely business perspective, public relations firms operate in a very interesting world. Few businesses are able to charge so much for their services and promise so little in return. Unfortunately, this is the reality of life when dealing with PR firms and publicists.

· · · · ·

Good firms charge a lot of money for their services, and they can't guarantee any results. Sure, they may guarantee a minimum number of radio show bookings or book reviews, but they can't guarantee that their efforts will translate into book sales.

One of the benefits of being published by a traditional publisher is that they will almost always have their own in-house PR team, or a contract publicist they work with for their books. But even so, some traditionally published authors choose to hire an outside firm to work with the publisher's team, and depending on the book, a publishing house may hire an outside firm as well.

If you self-publish, there are plenty of benefits to hiring an experienced publicist or PR firm: They will write all your press materials and will target the media outlets that are a good fit for you and your book.

Like editors, PR firms and contract publicists specialize in certain genres, and they usually will indicate which ones they are best suited for on their website. A primary reason for hiring a PR firm in your genre is that they should know right away which media outlets would be interested in a book like yours, and they should already have relationships with the people at those outlets. This will give them a leg up on getting you interviewed or your book reviewed.

Here is yet another case where having a good platform can really help you, as this will make it much easier for a publicist to get you exposure. This is because media outlets want to cover authors who already have a good following.

From a cost standpoint, a publicity campaign for a book from a good PR firm can be very expensive, starting from around $3,000 and going up. It's important to realize that you almost never see an immediate return on that investment. What I mean is that if you spend $3,000 on a PR campaign, you might need to sell something like 1,500 books just to break even (this example assumes a royalty of $2 per book as outlined in Tip #28). That $3,000 will be spent in a month or two, but it may take you several months to a year to sell that many books.

Of course, consider how many books you likely would have sold without this PR campaign. Unfortunately, this question is impossible to answer with accuracy. Now, if your publicist books you on Oprah's network or some other major national media, it's safe to say it was worth it! But since this almost never happens for first-time authors, we are left to evaluate the efforts with ambiguity.

If you do engage an outside firm, I strongly suggest you hire one that has experience in your genre and can provide references you can speak with. They should also provide some examples of their recent media placements for authors and books. Once you sign on with them, you should expect to receive a regular "hit report," which will provide details of which media outlets have agreed to do something with you or your book as a result of the firm's efforts.

In summary, if you have the money to spend and a book that makes sense for a PR campaign, and you are looking at it as a long-term investment in your career as an author and expert in your field, hiring a publicist to initiate a PR campaign is probably a good thing to do.

● ● ● ● ●

Marketing and Business

Start Selling Your Book *before* It's Published

Securing preorders is the best way to insure your book gets off to a fast start, and I work with all of my authors to conduct a preorder campaign with every book we publish. I strongly encourage you to do the same thing.

• • • • •

It doesn't matter whether you go with a traditional publisher or self-publish. Once you have a publication date and a book cover, you are ready to start promoting your book to your tribe. This will be the first test of the strength of your platform and how effectively you are reaching your audience.

In the case of a traditional publisher, your book will be available for preorder on Amazon and other e-tailers as well as the publisher's website a few months prior to publication.

I also suggest offering some incentives for readers to preorder, like an autographed copy via a bookplate. A bookplate is a fancy industry way of saying a plain white sticker that the author will autograph (and perhaps write a small message on) and mail to the reader so they may affix it inside their book. This allows the reader to order your book from anywhere and email you the proof of purchase, along with their mailing address. Once you have received their email and address, simply sign the bookplate and drop it in the mail.

Another option is to conduct a free teleclass on your book and make this available to anyone who preorders. With a variety of free conference call options available (see Tip #19), this will only cost you the time involved, and it will give readers a chance to connect with you and an incentive to order your book early.

Depending on your genre and situation, there may be other low-cost or no-cost things you can provide to those who preorder, so you will want to be creative here.

Whatever you decide, a preorder campaign has little downside, and if large orders start coming into Amazon and other e-tailers or brick-and-mortar bookstores before your book is even available, this will give bookstore buyers a reason to take notice and "order up" on your book.

● ● ● ● ●

Marketing and Business

What's the Best Way to Advertise Your Book?

Full disclosure: I must admit that my background in publishing began in the newspaper business, and I am well acquainted with most advertising mediums—especially traditional print advertising. As a result, I am not a fan of advertising books from an unknown author. For example, when is the last time *you* saw an ad for a book from an unknown author and purchased it as a result? In most cases, these ads don't produce sales for first-time authors.

For established authors, or "name brand" authors, advertising a book can certainly make sense. In this case, the author has such a strong following already that readers are willing to buy any book the author pens, so the ad serves more like a paid announcement that a new book is available rather than a traditional advertisement.

Too many times I see authors put their hopes in advertising for a book, because they see it as some sort of shortcut if they don't have a good platform. Let me be clear: *advertising your book is not a replacement for building your platform.*

If you have advertising dollars in your budget, you may want to spend that same amount of money on giving your book away! I realize this is distasteful to some authors, but I would ask you to reconsider that notion. Giving your book away in many cases is a far more effective use of your money than advertising because it can build a readership base for your book.

Goodreads.com, librarything.com, and other book-themed social media sites provide authors and publishers a vehicle to give a limited number of books away to readers who request them, with the only catch being the recipient of the free book has to read it and post a review about it. (See these websites for complete details.) If a reviewer really likes your book, hopefully they will refer it to someone else. In most cases, these book giveaways are much more effective for growing sales than standard advertising.

Business and Marketing

The Author Business Model

As we reach the end of this book, I want to share what I consider to be the most important tip if one of your goals is to make money as an author. From this moment forward, I want you to begin to think about your writing career in terms of what I call the Author Business Model.

•••••

Specifically defined, a good Author Business Model does not just take into account the writing and selling of a book, it also encompasses all the ways you can expand and monetize your sharing of information. There will be different options depending on your genre, but here is where you want to sit down, put your marketing hat on, and ask yourself: *What other products or offerings would my readers like to receive from me?*

Here are a few options:

- Paid lectures, workshops, and teleclasses can be an excellent source of revenue. When you first start out you will probably have to do these types of events at no charge, but there comes a point when, as they become well attended and you become proficient at giving them, you should begin charging. Payment could come in the form of admission fees from attendees or an honorarium from the host of your lecture or workshop.

- Private educational or coaching programs, small group intensive sessions, and phone/Skype consultations are other ways authors can earn money. Here, you provide an undivided portion of your time to share information and your expertise with an interested audience. This is an especially beneficial component for nonfiction authors who are presenting themselves as experts in their field.

- Workbooks, journals, and other written works that complement your primary book may also be an option (if you have signed with a traditional publisher, check your contract first to make sure you can do this). For example, Richard Bach, one of the best-selling fiction authors of all time, wrote a book called *Illusions*, which sold several million copies. He later published a book of selected quotations called *Messiah's Handbook*, which contained quotes that were very similar to those mentioned in *Illusions*.

- Are there any additional products that may be of interest to your readers? Hierophant author Sunny Dawn Johnston has created a whole line of angel cards and jewelry that she sells alongside her book at events, workshops, and on her website.

The more financially successful authors think like businesspeople, and many of the most financially successful authors I know actually make more from workshops and speaking engagements than they do from the royalties of their books!

In addition, a successful Author Business Model almost always includes more than one book. Many first-time authors have the idea that one book is going to generate enough money to sustain them, but that is almost never the case. As your tribe grows, so should your number of published books. In my opinion, a new book every two to three years is a good model to follow. This is another reason why you don't want to stuff everything you know into your first book; not only will it lack focus, but you also won't have anything left for subsequent books!

When it comes to a need for more than one book, you don't have to take my word for it. Simply look at every other successful author in the world, as they almost all have more than one book. (Harper Lee, author of *To Kill a Mockingbird*, is the one notable exception who comes to mind. So if your book wins the Pulitzer Prize and becomes required reading in public schools around the country, I guess one book is OK.)

Finally, while it may not make sense when you are first starting out, there comes a point when you should consult with a CPA in your home state to determine if it makes sense for you to set up a corporation or other legal entity to be the recipient of your royalties and other income associated from your author business.

Tax advice is well beyond the scope of this book, but the essential point I want to make here is that becoming an author is entering the publishing business, so make sure you approach it as such. A successful business endeavor includes thinking of all the ways you can grow revenue while keeping expenses at a minimum, and tax planning is a component of this.

So once again, here is another tip that gets back to the importance of marketing, platform building, and gaining a new understanding of the publishing industry as a whole. If you are going to make enough money at this, and dare I say enough money for it to be your only source of income, you will need to think of other ways to monetize the information you have presented.

I have purposely shared this tip with you at the end in the hopes that by the time you arrive here, you will have a good enough understanding of the publishing industry to see the importance of the Author Business Model, which ultimately is an incorporation of every other tip in this book.

Final Remarks

We have covered a lot of ground in these pages, much of which may be new to you. Many authors can feel overwhelmed after digesting all of these elements, especially when it comes to building an author platform.

There is one final thing I would like you to take away from this book as you enter the field of publishing, especially if you are feeling a bit overwhelmed right now: You can do this!

Don't listen to the naysayers who tell you otherwise. Remember to follow your heart, but also be willing to accept guidance and direction from those qualified to help you.

So when you can't find the inspiration to write the next chapter, or your workshop has only three people and you were hoping for thirty, remember, don't give up! Put one foot in front of the other, and if you keep implementing the strategies I have outlined in this book, good things will happen for you and your author business.

Most importantly, remember to have fun! You are doing this to help people, including yourself!

And now that you have reached the end, it's time for you to evaluate me. Did I follow my own tips in the creation of this book? Do you feel that the title accurately conveyed the contents? Did the cover represent the spirit of the book? Did I stay focused and explain things clearly? How did you learn about this book? From my platform? Was this book the result of a first or second generation sale?

I hope I passed, and I hope you found this crash course on publishing helpful.

I have just one final thing to share. If you implement all the tips in this book, develop a solid Author Business Model, and you feel your manuscript falls under the categories that we publish, I might just have a home for you and your books. That is my additional purpose for this book, to connect with new authors. Please visit the submissions page at www.hierophantpublishing.com to see if we are a good fit for you!

Until then, I encourage you to keep on writing, and, most importantly, to think like a publisher.

• • • • •

Acknowledgments

My entrance into the book side of the publishing industry was an unusual one for sure, but in keeping with my own advice, I will save that story for another book (my memoir!).

I must begin by thanking Bob Friedman and Frank DeMarco, cofounders of Hampton Roads Publishing, without whom I would not be here.

Next, I have learned much from my publishing colleagues Michael Kerber, Jan Johnson, Bonni Hamilton, and Caroline Pincus, all seasoned veterans of the industry who have produced wonderful books under the imprints of Weiser Books, Conari Press, Hampton Roads Publishing, and beyond.

I also wish to thank the people who helped produce this book and so many other Hierophant books, namely Allison Jacob, Jane Hagaman, Susie Pitzen, and Adrian Morgan. I am fortunate and grateful to work with such wonderful and talented people.

Lastly, but certainly not least, I must thank Greg Brandenburg, associate publisher at Hampton Roads, whom I am most indebted to for all his guidance and direction over the years, and who on more than one occasion has saved me from myself.

About the Author

Randy Davila is the president of Hierophant Publishing and Hampton Roads Publishing Company.

Between the two publishing houses, he has overseen the publication of books by authors such as don Miguel Ruiz Jr., Eckhart Tolle, Byron Katie, Neale Donald Walsch, Richard Bach, Jack Canfield, and many more. Randy regularly teaches author workshops at venues around the country. For his current lecture schedule, please visit www.insighteventsusa.com.

Randy graduated with distinction from the Classics, Philosophy, and Religion Department at the University of Mary Washington in Virginia, where he cofounded and wrote for the award-winning publication *The Free Press*. His spiritual short stories have received the Place of Peace Award. He lives in Boerne, Texas, with his wife Rachel, daughters Mia and Charlie, and their dog Teddy.

Hierophant Publishing
8301 Broadway, Suite 219
San Antonio, TX 78209
888-800-4240

www.hierophantpublishing.com